THE BANK CLERK WHO WENT TO WAR

MEMORIES OF A PROFESSIONAL CRICKETER

IAN ADDIS AND ANDREW RADD

WITH DAVID STEELE

Chequered Flag
PUBLISHING

First published in the UK by Chequered Flag Publishing 2018
PO Box 4669, Sheffield, S6 9ET
www.chequeredflagpublishing.co.uk

A CIP record for this book is available from the British Library

All images from David Steele collection unless stated

Printed in the EU by Print Group Sp. z o.o.

ISBN 978-1-9997774-3-2

For Steeles and Crumps
past, present and future

CONTENTS

FOREWORD

By Geoffrey Boycott

Cricket is a team game, but batting is for the individual within a team framework. In pressure situations, once you are in the middle nobody can help you. Your partner at the other end, your teammates in the dressing room, your best friends or your mum, are all of no use. You are on your own.

That's when you find out if you've got the bottle for a fight and find out that talent alone is not enough. Determination, mental toughness, concentration and patience are priceless.

Every cricketer soon learns that facing fast bowling and making runs is the hardest test for any batsman. That is why if my team was playing genuine pace or in a tough uphill battle I should want David Steele in my side because he had all the characteristics required to succeed.

I have played with too many batsmen who looked good in the nets but couldn't cut it when the going was hard. David's batting wasn't always pretty but you knew he loved the challenge. He was never going to shirk it no matter how difficult.

It's not always about playing beautiful shots and looking pretty. Sometimes the bowlers are so good they won't let you score quickly or play aesthetic strokes. Then it's about getting the job done.

As a lad growing up my uncle Algy always said to me, 'Stay in young'un. You can't make runs in the pavilion.' So I did. And so did David Steele.

My kind of batsman, full of character. I had great admiration for his batting.

INTRODUCTION

1975 AND ALL THAT

David Stanley Steele's brief but glorious brush with international cricket might never have happened if an England captain had taken more notice of the Birmingham weather forecast. Mike Denness won the toss in the first of four Tests against Australia in 1975, played at Edgbaston, and opted to bowl first. Various explanations were mooted at the time, but some good judges averred it was what would now be termed a 'negative insertion'. The forecasters were predicting rain in the coming days which exposed England to the risk of batting on a damp pitch. 'And this was exactly what happened,' recorded *Wisden*. 'The general opinion was that the England batsmen were not anxious to face [Dennis] Lillee and [Jeff] Thomson. They preferred to postpone the evil hour.'

In the event, Australia made a solid 359 all out. Then, moments after John Edrich and Dennis Amiss launched the home reply, a thunderstorm drenched the ground. When the players returned later on that fateful Friday afternoon, Lillee and Max Walker claimed seven wickets for 83 runs before the close and the match had been lost and won. England succumbed by an innings with a day and a half to spare and Tony Greig replaced Denness as captain for the second Test starting at Lord's just over a fortnight later. The team was to be announced on Sunday 27 July, when most of the first-class counties would be involved in 40-over John Player League matches.

David and his Northamptonshire teammates were travelling from Northampton – where they had started a Championship fixture against Mike Brearley's Middlesex on the Saturday – to play Worcestershire at Dudley. Jim Watts, the club's former (and future) captain, was sufficiently confident that his old friend and colleague would receive a first Test call to strike a £5 bet. David had made a highly promising start to the season but his three previous innings, including a double-failure against Greig's Sussex, produced just 22 runs. He agreed to the wager. Given his reputation for careful dealings in all matters financial (among his nicknames was 'Crime' because crime doesn't pay), it's a safe assumption that he didn't expect to lose his fiver. But lose it he did. At the age of thirty-three, David's dream of donning an England cap and sweater was about to come true. *Wisden* reckoned it 'a surprise choice' – but was it?

Since moving up the order to number three in 1971 – coinciding with Watts' elevation to the Northamptonshire captaincy for the first time – David had earned a name as one of the most reliable

'Take the fiver, Jim.' David pays Jim Watts his winnings.

run-scorers on the county circuit. The committee at Wantage Road valued him highly enough to award a benefit for the 1975 season, and his fellow professionals began speculating immediately about the effect this would have on his form. Batsman Alan Tait told David later that most of them were convinced he 'wouldn't do anything' that summer, such would be his determination to take full advantage of this once-in-a-career opportunity for a county journeyman to feather his nest for retirement. Everyone around the club knew he would do his damnedest to wring every last pound out of the punters. David admitted 'that's all I thought about, because if you didn't think about it you'd get bugger all. I picked a little benefit team, went out pretty much every night and just said to myself "I'll sleep when this year's over."' The old Glamorgan and England all-rounder Allan Watkins, then cricket professional at Oundle School, advised David along similar lines. The birth of his first child, Arran, in January 1975 focused the mind even more.

There was, of course, the traditional trap awaiting every beneficiary. Slog your guts out raffling bats in pubs, knocking over piles of pennies, chasing up articles and adverts for the brochure, organising cricket matches at local clubs, writing letters and generally pressing the flesh with the local business community, and you run the risk of losing form. Ducks and nought-for-plentys don't help the money-making cause. So you have to work even harder on the off-the-field stuff, making it more difficult still to churn out runs and wickets… and so on. With David, though, this was never an issue; his mind, he insisted, was 'clear as a bell, the concentration perfect' throughout the 1975 season.

His Souvenir Autograph Brochure (voluntary donation 20p) offers a clear insight into how hard he was prepared to graft to make the benefit a success. Four cricket matches – at Stony Stratford, Lilford Hall near Oundle and the villages of Boughton and Charlton – were scheduled in the space of just ten days, then a double-wicket competition at Milton Keynes, any number of discos and dances and, for the hungry punter, a barbecue evening at Rectory Farm in Great Addington: two quid a ticket and music from Icarus, 'the well-known

David's benefit year for Northamptonshire was interrupted by an international call up at the ripe old age of thirty-three.

group from the Midlands.' David was presumably absent from the benefit match at Raunds Town CC on the evening of 30 July on the grounds that he would be making his Test debut at Lord's the following morning.

Former England captains MJK Smith and Ray Illingworth contributed articles, as did his old Staffordshire mate (and future Derbyshire colleague) Bob Taylor. Alan Gibson, most readable of cricket writers, contributed some Northamptonshire memories 'in the cause of such a good cricketer and pleasant person as David Steele' while John Arlott praised him as the archetypal cricketing yeoman: 'he has deserved well of Northamptonshire and their supporters – the steady county cricketers of his kind maintain or domestic game.' The local reporter also had his say, Matthew Engle (sic) of the *Chronicle and Echo* considering the game's problematic financial state: 'It is thirteen years since Accrington Stanley gave up the ghost and disappeared from the Football League. So far no cricket side has had to follow suit; it would be nice to think that state of affairs will continue (but) these days no one can be quite sure.' David's own article reflected on his first twelve seasons at Wantage Road and expressed the hope that Northamptonshire would end 1975 as county champions. Worthy and predictable stuff. And there, portentously, on a couple of pages near the middle were photographs of Australian stars Dennis Lillee and Jeff Thomson, the high-profile tourists of the summer. And given his county form in recent seasons, some optimistic West Standers reckoned the beneficiary might not just be watching them on the telly in the weeks ahead.

The early indications were encouraging. Against Warwickshire at Northampton in mid-May he 'took on' former England fast bowler David Brown, and although the scorebook showed nothing exceptional – 36 in the first innings, 45 in the second – Dennis Amiss, playing for the opposition, pointed out to David that he was 'standing up' at the crease, giving a clear impression of confidence, rather than crouching over his bat in tense, nervous fashion. It was a telling observation by one wise and experienced pro to another. At the end of that month, Glamorgan came to Wantage Road and were promptly demolished by Sarfraz Nawaz and Bob Cottam for a paltry 89. Skipper Roy Virgin and Wayne Larkins both fell early but that brought Mushtaq Mohammad in to join David, and the pair carried the score to 180 for two by Saturday's close, Steele 79 not out and Mushtaq unbeaten on 73. On the Sunday, David hit three sixes in 69 against a strong Kent attack – Bernard Julien, Norman Graham, John Shepherd, Bob Woolmer and Derek Underwood – in the John Player League match at Tring in Hertfordshire, one of the outgrounds in Northamptonshire's cricketing hinterland. Then on Monday morning, David carried his Championship score to an unbeaten 126. He claimed years later it was probably the best he had ever batted – 'so clinical'. Then the pads came off and the benefit diary came out again to see where he was heading that night.

Another innings in the weeks leading up to his Test selection would live with him for decades, helping to fuel a sense of slow-burning injustice at his subsequent treatment by the men who picked him for England in the first place. Northamptonshire hosted Kent at Northampton and were left to make a highly improbable 367 to win in the fourth innings on a worn pitch – conditions ideally suited to Underwood's fizzing left-arm spin. The inevitable happened; all out for 138 with 'Deadly' harvesting five wickets for nine runs in a dozen well-nigh unplayable overs. But David made 84, 'masterly' said *Wisden*, to prevent a total rout. To anyone who witnessed it, a superbly skilful exhibition of batting craftsmanship, the suggestion that he was unlikely to succeed in spin-friendly conditions rang very hollow indeed. When eventually dismissed, caught around the corner by Brian Luckhurst off Underwood, he had to walk past Colin Cowdrey; hailed throughout his career as the exemplar of gentlemanly conduct and good sportsmanship. The great man had irritated David during Kent's first innings by standing his ground after an edge off Bob Cottam was safely pouched at slip. However, the catcher's successful appeal to umpire Don Oslear to 'give him out, I've caught it!' may have induced a wry smile from the outgoing batsman with David's reluctance to walk being well known on the county circuit.

Whatever the background, David took umbrage at what appears, certainly by modern standards, a mild enough send-off from Cowdrey – 'Catch it... next batsman, please!' – and the perceived slight still lingers. The batsman's aggrieved reaction confused Cowdrey who enquired of Luckhurst, 'What's wrong with David? That's not like him.'

Looking back David recalls the incident with remarkable clarity.

'What's wrong with David? 84 runs on an unplayable wicket and he comes out with, "Catch it... next batsman, please!" But we shook hands at the close with no hard feelings.'

After the disaster at Edgbaston, the new Test skipper made a point of talking to county umpires about players worth considering for Lord's. Barry Wood and Bob Woolmer, as well as David, came into the side. A fiver worse off, David battled his way to 44 not out in the Sunday league at Dudley – New Zealander Glenn Turner smashing 30 runs off an eight-ball over from John Dye to hasten the finish – before Mike Selvey, an England choice the following summer, removed him for a single in the second innings of the Championship match against Middlesex, which Northamptonshire lost by five wickets. Next stop St John's Wood, carrying with him his precious fits-like-a-slipper kit, taken from the car park at a benefit match in Wellingborough a couple of weeks earlier but then returned following publicity in the local press.

David would later claim the atmosphere in England's dressing room at Lord's was 'not confident' despite the change of leadership. Greig had personality and charisma, a cricketing gladiator, and he wanted the Northamptonshire man in his team. But several of the players who reported for duty at headquarters had come through an ordeal by fire in Australia the previous winter, losing the series 4-1 (the solitary victory coming in the dead-rubber final Test) after Denness had dropped himself from the team at Sydney, Edrich filling the breach and suffering cracked ribs for his efforts. To lift the mood, Eric Morecambe and Ernie Wise, Britain's best-loved double act then

The England team with whom David made his debut.
Back: Bob Woolmer, Graham Gooch, Chris Old, Peter Lever, Dennis Amiss, David Steele, Barry Wood. Front: John Snow, Alan Knott, Tony Greig, John Edrich, Derek Underwood.

at the peak of their TV popularity as the official makers-or-breakers of Christmas day for a hefty chunk of the British population, were invited in for a morale-boosting visit. Eric got a laugh by taking one look at Amiss's hairy chest and quipping 'you weren't born, you were trapped!' The pavilion attendant came in with a pile of clean towels, and David stuck to his usual practice of selecting one to use as a thigh pad. Saves a few bob, and more comfortable, he always reckoned.

When Greig went out to toss with Ian Chappell on the morning of Thursday 31 July, David was hoping the Australian skipper would call correctly and put England in the field. An easier introduction. But it wasn't to be. Greig won the toss and opted to bat, no 'postponing the evil hour' with him. Wood and Edrich went in first, and with only ten runs on the board the former perished to Lillee, the first of five leg-before decisions given in the tourists' favour during the innings. David's moment had come.

Much of what followed has passed into cricket folklore, starting with his delayed entrance after going down one flight of stairs too many in the pavilion, accustomed as he was to using the 'away' rather than the 'home' dressing room at Lord's, and ending up in the lavatory where the attendant felt obliged to point out that he wouldn't score many runs in there. But he was 'floating on air' on his way out to the middle, before a gaggle of Australians – including umpire Bill Alley – brought him back to earth. Was it Groucho Marx, pondered the opposition? Or maybe Father Christmas? David was marginally relieved to be facing Lillee rather than Thomson first up: 'Dennis's beautiful, classic action was right for you as a batsman – always on line, never down the leg-side. Thommo's slinging action from wide of the crease was more difficult.' Noting Lillee leaning on Alley's shoulder at the other end, he asked for his guard – 'Bill, can we have a game of cricket?' – and told himself over and over again to 'watch the ball'. Two blocks, a leave, and then a short ball pulled away for four. The crowd in the ground, and the millions watching at home, liked what they saw.

'Feel better now?' asked Edrich as they met in the mid-pitch. David felt calm, in his element because there was a bat in his hand

*Taking guard in the toilets –
a lighthearted take on David
getting lost in the pavilion
on his way to the crease.*

MIDDLE AND
LEG, PLEASE!

and runs that needed to be scored. Soon Edrich, Amiss and young Graham Gooch, who had bagged a pair on debut at Edgbaston, were back in the pavilion. At 49 for four England's new captain walked out to join one of his own picks. The pair saw it through to lunch and afterwards two milestones beckoned – David's fifty and the century partnership. The first duly arrived when a short ball from off-spinner Ashley Mallett was worked away for a single to the fielder on the midwicket boundary. But with the stand worth 96, David played what he described as his 'worst bloody shot of the season', miscuing an attempted pull and dragging the ball into his stumps. DS Steele, bowled Thomson, 50. Two hours and forty-three minutes at the crease, 109 balls, nine fours. It meant he was highly unlikely to go down in the record books as a one-Test wonder, but at the same time he knew he hadn't seen the job through. Long after his retirement from the game it still kept him awake at night, or else haunted his dreams. Once in his slumbers he reached the 90s, got up for a drink of water, went back to sleep again hoping to reach three figures this time, and discovered his score had ticked back to 50.

In the world of the wide awake, England totalled 315 – Greig falling for 96 – and then had the Australians reeling at 133 for eight before Ross Edwards, Lillee and Mallett engineered a recovery to 268 all out. The two bowlers added 69 frustrating runs for the last wicket until Greig turned to his new talisman and David pinned Mallett in front with his fourth ball in Test cricket. Another 45 runs in the second innings, another irritating dismissal (skewing a leading edge back to dibbly-dobbler medium-pacer Dougie Walters, a renowned partnership-breaker) and another wicket – opener Rick McCosker lbw as Australia batted out for a draw – added up to an eminently satisfactory debut.

And he was the story. A cartoonist's dream with his steel-rimmed specs, grey hair and cap with the peak turned up, for which there was a reason. Wearing glasses, the heat would make it feel 'like a fish and chip shop' with a conventional peak, hence the jockey look. The most famous sports cartoonist of them all, Roy Ullyett of the *Daily Express*, made David the main subject of his offering in the next day's newspaper, suggesting the selectors might now consider selecting any batsman wearing a monocle, pince-nez, lorgnette or even a telescope. Best of all, David had been presented to Her Majesty the Queen during the tea interval on the first day. 'I'd seen it on the telly, the two lines of players drawn up, and there I was.' Of the many photographs in his personal archive, that remains the most prized.

David hadn't finished with the Australians, either. A few days after the Lord's Test he was facing them again, on this occasion in Northamptonshire colours. The tour match at Wantage Road attracted a handy crowd, boosted undoubtedly by David's recent heroics – plus the chance to buy one of the new 'Cricket's a Big Hit!' T-shirts from the shop under the scorers' and press box – and after falling to Max Walker for 29 in the first innings he made the century (102 with fifteen fours) that the County Ground faithful had come to see. During that game another component of the Steele legend fell into place when Mike Buswell, of the wholesale meat firm Dalgety

Buswell, agreed to sponsor David in kind for his Test performances: one lamp chop for every run up to 50, and then a chop and a steak for every run thereafter. After another successful outing in the third Test at Headingley – 73 and 92 – Buswell sent David a telegram suggesting he might go easy for a bit because their lamb stocks were running low. When that match was abandoned on the fifth day following vandalism of the pitch carried out by campaigners for the release of George Davis, imprisoned for armed robbery, some of his teammates tried to convince David that his runs – and thus his chops and steaks – would be deemed null and void. It was also the game that saw Woolmer, performing twelfth man duties, obliged to carry out a few safety pins to hold a particularly venerable pair of David's batting trousers together.

The series ended at The Oval with David playing his part in a notable England rearguard action. Following on 341 runs adrift with nearly three days remaining – this was a six-day Test because the outcome of the series was still undecided – England managed to bat until tea on the final day to draw the game. David and John Edrich added 125 for the second wicket before Woolmer, back in the team on cricketing merit rather than taking responsibility for invisible mending, carved out a six-and-a-half-hour century. David recalls Lillee booking an early flight home on the fifth day but having to cancel it because England were still at the crease. Knocks of 39 and 66 gave David 365 runs at 60.83, the top of the averages in his maiden Test series, and filled the Steele freezer with meat for the foreseeable future. The trophy cabinet too, as a welter of awards and accolades came his way. There were frequent references to the spirit of 1940: 'All that was missing was the ARP helmet,' said Frank Keating in the *Guardian*, recalling David's finest hour at the time of his retirement nearly a decade later. The peerless sitcom *Dad's Army* was almost as popular as Morecambe and Wise at the time, and journalists were not slow to make comparisons with Captain Mainwaring or even Lance-Corporal 'Don't Panic!' Jones. But Clive Taylor of *The Sun* produced the phrase that best summed up the appeal of Britain's latest sporting hero – 'the bank clerk goes to war'.

There was still, though, a season to finish with Northamptonshire – and an odd one it had been for the club. 'The summer of four captains' began with Virgin appointed to lead the side. He lasted until the end of July, but it wasn't the job for him so Watts – who had resigned at the end of the previous season to train as a teacher – took the helm again. He lasted a week before breaking a finger on the opening day of the county's match against the Australians, leaving a leadership vacuum for the following day's Sunday league game with Glamorgan at Wellingborough School. On television, too. Thus it was that David led the Northamptonshire side out of the thatched pavilion on The Grove. Tradition has it that success on this attractive ground can be guaranteed by stepping on WG Grace's doorstep, salvaged from the Old Man's demolished home in Bristol shortly before the Second World War by cricket-mad schoolmaster Murray Witham and placed in front of the pavilion in 1940. You can only deduce that David stepped over it this time. Pakistan's Majid Khan whacked the bowling to all parts – David, trying himself as second-change, conceding 40 runs in five overs – and reached his fifty from just 22 balls,

The Sec, Ken Turner, hands over part of the proceeds from a successful benefit season.

then the fastest half-century in the competition's history. The acting skipper then nicked behind off Malcolm Nash as Northamptonshire plummeted to defeat by 148 runs. For the team's next Championship fixture, at Bournemouth, Mushtaq took charge, retained the role for the rest of the season and the appointment was duly made substantive for 1976. It wasn't a job David wanted, and as we shall see his only spell as a fully-fledged county captain – at Derbyshire rather than Northamptonshire – was not a roaring success. Certainly in the closing weeks of '75 he had other priorities, not least keeping that all-important benefit diary up-to-date...

PART ONE

SETTING THE TYPE

I

THE STEELES

David's father, Alfred, was born in 1906 and grew up in the Staffordshire pit village of Bucknall near Hanley, one of the six towns that comprise the city of Stoke-on-Trent. Despoiled by coalfields, polluted with the smoke from hundreds of pottery kilns, the area was, in the words of JB Priestley, 'an exceptionally mean, dingy provinciality of Victorian industrialism in its dirtiest and most cynical aspect.' The second child of Ernest and Hannah Steele, Alfred was destined to follow his father down the mines and would spend almost all his working life in the coal industry before taking early retirement at the age of sixty – a decision that almost certainly prolonged his life by many years. Shortly before his death a consultant told him that fifty per cent of his lungs were impaired by silicosis. 'More like 100 per cent,' he replied.

The Steeles lived in a four-roomed cottage in Werrington Road, which became increasingly cramped as the family grew. By 1918 it comprised four boys; George, Alfred, Ernest and Wilfred, and two girls, Hilda and Anne. Unlike his brothers and sisters, Alfred left the family home following his mother's early death in 1920 and went into lodgings in nearby Werrington. He was fourteen years old. Soon he was walking six miles to the pit head every day, returning in the evening blackened and grimy to await the kettle boiled on the range and eventual immersion in the ubiquitous tin bath – it would be several years before his local coalfield was blessed with the luxury of pit head baths. It was dangerous work for a young lad. The hazardous nature of life underground, with the ever present danger of explosion, flooding, suffocation or fire, is reflected in the eighteen fatalities recorded in the North Staffordshire coalfields during Alfred's first year of work.

Unusually, given their background, none of Alfred's brothers went down the mine. The eldest, George, went into the Grenadier Guards. He was, by reputation, a dour, humourless man. David recalls his father describing a trip to The Scratch, the local cinema, which was showing a Laurel and Hardy film.

'What are you laughing at?' George asked as Alf's shoulders rocked. 'What's so funny?'

'If you can't laugh at this you'll never laugh,' Alf replied.

Father and mother, Alfred and Grace Steele.

And he never did, retaining his gloomy demeanour into old age when, at a family funeral he accosted David and sombrely enquired, 'You'll come to mine, won't you?'

David replied, straight-faced, 'Yes, Uncle George, I'll go to yours.'

Alf had little to do with Ernest, a jobbing gardener with a strong liking for the drink. Alf was strictly, fiercely even, teetotal, originating from a strong Methodist background and exposure to the heavy drinking culture of the pit village, where he witnessed workers pouring hard-earned money down their throats and the distressing, often violent, aftermath of drunkenness. Many years later, when accompanying younger son John, the Leicestershire opening batsman, on a coaching trip to South Africa he was offered a drink in a bar.

'I'll have an orange juice,' Alf replied.

'Have a pint of beer, it'll do you good.'

'An orange juice,' he insisted.

'Come on, get a pint down you.'

At this point he squared up to his benefactor. 'Am I any less a man than you because I don't drink?'

He got his orange juice.

David further describes his father as a quiet, highly principled man, self-disciplined, determined and obdurate – qualities that many a frustrated bowler would recognise in his son.

The youngest brother, Wilf, notably well spoken with no hint of a Staffordshire accent, went into the RAF and then became a sales director for a wine company based in Peterborough. David recalled phone conversations with his uncle and the invitation to 'call and see us just before Christmas with a few samples'.

Sister Anne married her cousin, Fred Steele, and settled in High Lane, near Chell, while the glamorous 'come and give me a squeeze' Hilda moved with her husband to Manchester before returning to charm customers while waitressing in a restaurant in Hanley.

Having moved out of the family home at the age of fourteen, Alf's partial estrangement from the Steeles was compounded by his father's re-marriage. However, membership of the local chapel provided succour and support and it was there that Alf met, courted and even-

Brothers in arms: John and David at home in Brown Edge.

tually married Grace Crump. Despite his mother-in-law's apparent displeasure – 'not another bloody miner!' – he was warmly welcomed into the Crump family circle.

Alf and Grace settled at 134 High Lane, Brown Edge and had two boys, David born in 1941 and John five years later.

The village offered a stable and secure environment and several friendships David forged during schooldays have survived the passing years. Memories, too, are etched deeply. Mining communities were no strangers to tragedy, but the death of a child remained a shocking event. Almost seventy years have passed since a classmate, Gerald Shelcross, ran into the road and was struck by an LMS lorry, but David has a vivid recollection of the accident and still visits the little boy's grave on his occasional returns to Brown Edge.

Brown Edge had its own school, church, Methodist chapel, Co-operative store and two butcher's shops, one of which, Harrison's, was the village meeting place. David often accompanied his mother on shopping trips to purchase the regular 'undercut of the rump, please, Les,' for 12/6. It was there he encountered Mrs Proctor, mother of triplets, and owner of the broadest Staffordshire accent he'd ever heard. Turner's Buses ran a local return service into Hanley, but occasionally it would offer a day's excursion to more exotic destinations.

'Are you going on the trip to Manchester on Wednesday?' asked Mrs Steele.

'Yes,' replied Mrs Proctor. 'I'll leave our Pim and Nev a piece of meat and a big bowl of peas and they can fart to their hearts content.'

One-legged Sam Pratt ran the other butcher's. Returning home on his motorbike after a night on the beer, he had collided with a level crossing barrier and paid the price. He and his wife were childless, but he won the affection of the village children with a Friday afternoon ritual when he would gather all the loose change from his till and throw it into the street outside the shop for the excited youngsters to collect.

One of the concessions afforded to miners in the early post-war years was a free ton of coal, delivered and tipped in a great heap outside the front gate. This would then be bucketed laboriously up the garden path and into the coalhouse. One day David discovered that Harry Turner, the next door neighbour, had his coal delivered in bags and raised the matter with his father.

'Why are we spending hours loading and moving the loose coal when he just shifts the bags?'

'He pays half a crown for the privilege,' an ever-prudent Alf replied, 'so it'll be buckets for us.'

Alf wasn't easily parted from his money. Two of his great pleasures were to watch Stoke City during the winter and Norton Miners' Welfare cricket in the summer. One Saturday afternoon he was sitting in his usual place on the boundary when Norton's professional, the former Indian Test player Gulabrai 'Ram' Ramchand, made a half-century. To mark such occasions, a common practice at the time was for a club official to walk around the ground with a money box requesting donations. When he reached Alf, he shouted, 'Collection for the professional!'

Alf's response was curt. 'Move on,' he said, adding pointedly, 'I'd contribute for an amateur, not a professional.'

*

David attended the local infant and junior schools before progressing to Endon Secondary Modern. It seems inconceivable, given his remarkable success as a cricketer, that he had few opportunities to play the game at school. The only time he handled a cricket bat at junior school was when a glass cabinet in the school hall was opened and a polished Gunn and Moore handed among the boys like a museum exhibit. The assistant headteacher at Endon, Spencer Eardley, was a 'cricket man' who played regularly for Bignal End in the North Staffs League and gave David welcome encouragement and advice when a career in the game was discussed, but little cricket was played. Football ruled the roost all the year round and David was both keen and talented. He had pedigree. For a generation of Stoke City supporters the name Steele was synonymous with David's Uncle Fred.

Freddie 'Nobby' Steele joined the Potters in 1931 and made his first team debut three years later at the age of eighteen. In 1936-37 he

England's other ball sport: the 1953-54 Endon Secondary Modern football team. David sits on the front row holding the ball.

was the First Division top scorer with thirty-three goals in thirty-five league games, a club record. That same season he won six international caps, scoring eight goals, including a hat-trick against Sweden and England's solitary goal in a 3-1 defeat by Scotland. That match, played at Hampden Park, Glasgow, attracted a crowd of 149,547, a record attendance in Britain. His Stoke City teammate and friend Stanley Matthews was on England's right wing that afternoon. Matthews was effusive in his praise for Fred, recalling in his autobiography that 'in the penalty box he was lethal, clinical and merciless, firing in shots from the tightest of angles and the smallest of spaces ... a masterpiece of strength, endurance, polish and skill that more often than not resulted in a billowing net.'

Fred also displayed a remarkable level of commitment. A serious knee injury sustained early in the 1937-38 season ended his international career, but he recovered to play a crucial role in Stoke's struggle against relegation later in the campaign. Victory in the final match at home to Liverpool on Saturday 7 May was essential to First Division survival. It also just happened to be Fred's wedding day. Racing from

Uncle Freddie Steele (centre), a Stoke City legend.

the ceremony, he reached the ground in time to take his place in the side and cap a most memorable day by scoring the second goal in the 2-0 win that secured the vital points.

Alf was a regular at the Victoria Ground, David joining him on the terrace in the late 1940s to watch his uncle in action. Like so many of his generation, the war had interrupted Fred's playing career, but after combining life as an army physical training instructor with guesting for a host of football clubs up and down the country, he returned to the Potteries for the first post-war season. In April 1946 he travelled to Iceland to manage KR Reykjavik, taking charge of the Icelandic national team in its first ever international match against Denmark that July. Although he returned to Stoke in time for the new English season, the managerial experience would prove invaluable. Released by Stoke in 1949, Fred became player-manager of Mansfield before moving to Port Vale in a similar role two years later. Under his leadership, the Valiants enjoyed their most successful season in the club's long history when winning the Third Division North title in 1953-54. Their exploits re-wrote the Football League record books: twenty-six goals conceded in a season of forty-six games, only five conceded at home, thirty clean sheets; but it was their FA Cup run that captured the nation's imagination.

David was amongst the crowd of 42,000 at Vale Park for the fifth round tie against Blackpool and Fred's old teammate, Stanley Matthews, when his uncle's shrewd deployment of quick, powerful tacklers and neat, skilful attackers helped defeat his First Division opponents. Two goals from Albert Leake saw the Valiants through and, after beating Leyton Orient in round six, they met West Bromwich Albion in the semi-final. However, there was no fairytale ending, the Albion coming from a goal behind to win 2-1. Unfortunately the remarkable level of success could not be maintained. After two mediocre Second Division campaigns, and with relegation a distinct possibility, Fred resigned as manager in January 1957. He returned to Vale Park in the early sixties for a brief spell but was unable to repeat his earlier triumphs and left by mutual consent in February 1965.

An inspirational personality in the dressing room and years ahead of his time in tactical awareness, Fred always had difficulty managing his nervous disposition, often watched games from the treatment room rather than at pitch-side and, superstitiously, sported black and white hooped football socks under his suit while wearing his trademark tweed trilby hat – the same hat he doffed so courteously to David's aunt Anne when courting in Hanley years before. As a young man, David would visit Fred in his cottage in Porthill and encourage him to tell tales of his sporting past – not an easy task as he was modest, unassuming and didn't give much away. As David reflects, 'I don't think he realised just how famous he was.'

David's own hopes of following his illustrious uncle into a career in professional football were dashed when he broke his leg one Saturday morning whilst playing for Leek schoolboys against Runcorn in an English Schools Cup match. A collision with the onrushing goalkeeper resulted in a greenstick fracture and a long journey to the local hospital, only to find that by the time they arrived, the orthopaedic department was closed. The leg was bandaged and put in a primitive splint and it wasn't until Monday, after a painful weekend, that corrective treatment could be applied.

The injury put paid to a trial with West Bromwich Albion, arranged for the following week, and left him with serious ligament damage. His doctor's words proved prescient.

'You'd be better sticking to cricket now.'

2

THE CRUMPS

David's mother was a coal miner's daughter. Her father, Fred, born in Barnsley in 1883, had moved to Staffordshire with his family and by 1901 was living in Smallthorne, near Burslem, and working at Sneyd Colliery. He married Hannah Frost in 1908 and they had four children. Reginald became the manager of the Co-operative Store in David's village of Brown Edge, Stanley worked as a smithy at the Sneyd pit before moving into the ceramics industry, Lilian married Bill Hughes, a textile worker, and lived in Leek, while Grace became Mrs Alfred Steele.

Fred and Hannah had settled at 62 Hayes Street, Bradeley, a soot-encrusted, red-brick terraced house, which became a focal point for their extended family every Sunday during the early post-war years. Alfred, Grace and David, with baby John in a pusher, walked the five miles from Brown Edge while Stan, wife Jennie and David's cousin Brian made a similar journey from their home in Chell.

The crowded living room resounded to the chatter of three generations, the younger members in awe of their grandfather whose photograph stared down from its prized position on the wall. Fred Crump was a man of his time. When he returned home from work the sound of his hand on the back door latch was the signal for Hannah to drain the boiled potatoes. Memories of those distant Sundays remain vivid with the blackened grate, the hessian-backed rag rug, the hymns on the wireless, the aroma of baking, the shuffling of cards and the familiar cribbage mantra – 'fifteen two, fifteen four, two's six and one for his knob' – and the endless cricket talk.

David's father, Alf, loved sport and was a keen spectator, but the Crumps were cricketers. Fred had opened the batting and kept wicket for Norton Miners' Welfare in the North Staffordshire League. Nicknamed 'Stonewall' Crump, his bat-and-pad-forward style slowly accumulated runs as he patiently amassed a score. His most memorable innings, and the one of which he was proudest, was a century achieved against the great SF, Sydney Francis Barnes, who was then professional for Porthill Park.

Barnes was the colossus of Staffordshire cricket and an inspiration to generations of players from the county. His phenomenal skill and appetite for getting batsmen out helped Staffordshire win six Minor Counties Championship titles from 1906 to 1927, and his record for them of over 1,400 wickets at just over eight runs apiece simply takes the breath away. Opponents who made runs against him dined out

A family tradition: grandfather Fred Crump, seated second from left, with Norton CC c.1910.

on it for years; Billy Kingston, a sports outfitter from Northampton, scored a match-winning century for David's future county at Stoke in 1904 and it's still reckoned to be among the finest innings ever played for the club. Barnes was a regular member of the England team between 1901 and 1914, playing twenty-seven matches and taking 189 wickets at an average of 16.43. Many good judges still rate him among the greatest bowlers in cricket history. Sadly for the first-class scene he made a limited number of appearances for Warwickshire and Lancashire, preferring life as a well-paid mercenary in league and Minor Counties cricket. Starting his career with Rishton in the Lancashire League in 1895, he was engaged as a professional in every season (with the exception of 1939) until his retirement from playing in 1940 at the age of sixty-seven. He made his first appearance for Staffordshire in 1904 and his last, along with Fred Crump's son Stanley and the seventeen-year-old Jack Ikin, against Yorkshire Seconds in 1935. A testimonial match to commemorate his eightieth birthday took place on Sunday, 26 April 1953, and cricketers from far and near, including England players Bill Edrich, Denis Compton, Eric Hollies and Norman Yardley came to do homage to him. Remarkably, Sydney changed into his flannels and, sporting his famous green Staffordshire cap, bowled an opening over of immaculate length and accuracy against Ikin, his former protégé. It was a maiden.

Grandfather Fred may have carved David's first little wooden bat and bowled at him in the yard behind the Hayes Street cottage, but his great mentor and the most important influence on his approach to the game, was Uncle Stanley. An accomplished cricketer, Stanley Crump was an all-rounder who batted at five or six, bowled, and fielded in the slips. His playing career began when, aged just twelve and the scorer for Norton Seconds, he was called into action when someone failed to turn up. Within two years he was a regular in the second team until a period of unemployment following the General Strike of 1926 severed his connection with Norton and he moved on to Chell Cricket Club and a job in the nearby colliery. Stanley was first selected for Staffordshire in 1930 and continued to represent his county for the next thirty years. In 1931 he was appointed as profes-

Staffordshire stalwart,
Uncle Stanley Crump.

sional at Caverswall before moving to Porthill and into the Central Lancashire League for stints with Rochdale and Leyland Motors. After the war he continued in the North Staffs League, combining league appearances with games for Staffordshire in the Minor Counties Championship before ending his career with the Newcastle Club playing alongside nephew David, who was then the club professional.

Stanley's attitude was founded on a number of simple principles. As a batsman he got his head down, got to the pitch of the ball and got behind it. Defence may have been his priority, but he could quickly appraise the bowling and any weaknesses were punished with a variety of attacking strokes. David recalls a towering six, swept over square leg from a kneeling position, when playing for Staffordshire against Cheshire at Crewe. He could also vary his bowling, delivered with the same beautiful action adopted by son, Brian, mixing seam and off-spin as conditions required. It was his character that underpinned his success. The determination not to lose, to give the opposition nothing, was inherited from his father who was his severest critic. But fundamental was his sheer love of the game. He never smoked, never drank and spent every winter practising, every summer playing, until he finally hung up his old Staffordshire cap at the age of sixty.

For almost forty years Stanley Crump was a leading light in North Staffs, one of the most competitive and highly rated leagues outside the first-class game. It attracted large attendances at matches and generous coverage in the *Stoke Sentinel* where the clubs' fortunes were followed avidly by a wide readership. No doubt interest was sustained by the lengthy list of famous names who gave their services as professionals. David's first club, Norton Miners' Welfare, employed former West Indian test player Manny Martindale in 1952, but he was just the forerunner of a talented line. The following year Frank Worrell joined the club. David's admiration of the great West Indian goes

A youthful Brian Crump, cousin of David, meets the great SF Barnes with Denis Haynes (Staffordshire captain) and Frank Crompton (Minor Counties Honorary Secretary).

beyond appreciation of his cricketing talent: 'He was class as a batter, class as a person. A real presence, graceful, elegant and the role model for later players like Vivian Richards and Brian Lara'. Worrell was succeeded by England star Jim Laker, the Australian Cec Pepper and then, from 1964-67, Sir Garfield Sobers. Commenting on Sobers' association with his old club, former Derbyshire player Peter Gibbs wrote in the 2014 edition of *Wisden*, 'It seems the stuff of make-believe ... Today the stars are beamed to us by satellite as they follow a globe-trotting schedule far removed from the colliery environs of Norton Cricket Club.'

Stanley's appetite for the game was insatiable. Frustrated by the lack of facilities in the days before indoor cricket schools he constructed, with the help of willing hands, a practice wicket in the back yard of his home at 52 Burlidge Road, Chell Green. Twenty tons of soil and rock had to be excavated before the necessary hardcore could be spread and concrete laid. Wire netting provided a rudimentary safety screen to protect the neighbours from the occasional misdirected hockey ball, bouncier than its red-leather counterpart and easier to pick up in the fading light. The respected cricketing journalist, Alex Bannister, writing in the May 1976 edition of *The Cricketer International,* reflected on the family's devotion to the cause: 'Cold, rain, fog and snow – many's the time the pitch had to be swept clear – were ignored. Slightly potty and eccentric? Of course.'

Stan was practical too. On particularly cold afternoons he wore pyjamas under his shirt, sweater and flannels. Familiar opponents would show the bulky figure striding to the wicket wearing his Staffordshire cap at a jaunty angle their utmost respect. Others might snigger, incredulously, rather like those Aussies gathered on the square at Lord's on that fateful day in 1975, and play on to regret it.

Stanley's knowledge, skills and enthusiasm were infectious and he brought these qualities to his coaching. For Brian, and nephews David and John, his credibility was enhanced by their playing with and watching him in action. Like all the best teachers, it was, 'don't just do as I say, do as I do.' And to his great credit all three enjoyed successful careers in the first-class game.

3

APPRENTICESHIPS

David served two apprenticeships, concurrently, from 1955 to 1962. At the age of fourteen he made his first appearance for Norton Cricket Club in the Kidsgrove Under 18 League against a Chell team which included seventeen-year-old old Brian Crump, and *his* cousin, Derek Smith, a medium-pace bowler. Playing in front of a crowd, with his mother and Aunt Jennie prominent, it was an inauspicious debut memorable only for a ball from young Smith which reared up from a length and struck David a glancing blow on the head.

'It was the first and last time,' David reflects with more than a hint of pride. 'I played against the world's fastest, mostly without a helmet, and was never hit on the head again.' He was struck on the ear, though, years later by Surrey bowler Robin Jackman.

The Kidsgrove League, which survives today, was a perfect proving ground for aspiring young cricketers. Matches were played on Monday evenings, starting at 6.30pm and, as David lived some seven miles from the ground in Norton, presented transport difficulties in those days before every family owned a car or two. The team was supervised by Albert Leake, a North Staffs League cricketer and scorer of the goals which beat mighty Blackpool in Uncle Freddie's Port Vale side of 1954, who acted as general manager and umpire.

Perhaps the most bizarre game in which David ever took part was an away match against Crewe Rolls Royce later that year. Having been put in to bat, Crewe were dismissed for just two runs, neither of which came off the bat. Both were leg byes. Graham Lord took five for none, left-arm spinner Steele, four for none and there was one run out. The runs were knocked off with one hit and within an hour of the game starting, Norton were back on the coach and homeward bound.

By 1956 David was ready to leave Endon Secondary Modern and enter the world of work. He had ambitions to make a career in professional cricket but his father, ever aware of pitfalls, said, 'Get a trade to your back. Your cousin Crumpy's done well in printing. Give that a go.'

Heeding his father's advice, David enrolled on a course at Stoke School of Art to learn the rudiments of typesetting and design and

A well-worn souvenir of David's early years in cricket – a photograph showing several luminaries of the Staffordshire League including Garry Sobers.

then responded to an advertisement for an apprentice compositor at Warwick Savage's Wedgwood Press in Burslem. After a successful interview with shop floor manager, Cyril Harvey, he was offered a job at the princely sum of £2 per week.

David's cricketing apprenticeship took a step forward when he moved from Norton to Sneyd, where Stanley Crump was the club professional. After beginning in the seconds, under the captaincy of one Derek Smith, he soon graduated to the first team. His progress was enhanced by exposure to a strict regime, imposed by his uncle but with David's wholehearted compliance. This involved taking his cricket gear in to work in Burslem, meeting his uncle out of his factory in Pot Bank at the end of the day, walking a mile to the cricket ground in Sneyd, putting up the nets, practising all evening, taking the nets down, and then walking home – three nights a week. Such dedication was rewarded by a consistent improvement in technique and produced noteworthy performances with both bat and ball. He hit his maiden century at Crewe LMR whose professional, seam bowler Dennis Cox, was formerly at Surrey. Particularly memorable was a half-century scored against the wiles of the great West Indian spinner Sonny Ramadhin, one of 'those little pals of mine' (with Alf Valentine) during the 1950 Test series against England, then professional at Ashcombe Park.

David recalls him 'taking the new cherry, unwrapping it, and bowling the first ball, which turned square. You could hear it buzzing in its flight. Incredible.' David's next confrontation with the legendary Ram was at Old Trafford in May 1964. Ramadhin took five for 82 in Northamptonshire's first innings but David was not among his victims. He top scored with 72 before falling to the medium-pace of Ken Higgs.

Who said he couldn't play spinners?

A first hat-trick was achieved against a Norton side which included Frank Worrell, although the great man's wicket eluded David. No doubt, on his return home, his mother took one look at his tongue and gave her customary greeting: 'You took some wickets today, lad.' Like many of the grounds in the North Staffs League the pitch was founded on coal. Fondling the ball and licking his spinning fingers before delivery, David's hands would become blackened with coal dust – a sure sign that he'd been busy that afternoon.

At Sneyd David appeared alongside club professionals; Indian Antoo Palwankar, Trinidadian Oliver Demming and Jim Edmonds, once on the professional staff at Northamptonshire – further evidence of the strength of the league at that time.

In 1960, at the tender age of nineteen, David was encouraged by Uncle Stan to apply for the vacant post of professional at Newcastle and Hartshill CC. He got the job and was paid £5 a week, twice as much as he received at the printers. The money was not squandered but put away for future use. As he was still without his own transport, the club generously agreed to underwrite his taxi fare to and from games. The investment proved a shrewd one, and during his first season in 1961 he scored useful runs and took seventy wickets.

Sneyd CC in 1960 featuring nineteen-year-old David Steele.
Back: Stan Powell, Tony Harrison, Alan Rogerson, Vernon Owen, Ken Brown, Terry Harrison. Front: David Steele, Jim Edmonds, Jesse Hall, Eric Hillwood, Graham Barnett.

His efforts earned a wage increase of thirty bob the following season, but the real bonus came when Stanley Crump, then a sprightly fifty-two year old, joined the club. It was a fruitful partnership. Their bowling combination, described in simple terms by Uncle Stan as 'I'll bowl the left handers out, you bowl the right,' was hugely effective and elevated the team to the top of the league.

The pair enjoyed particular success in the vital match against title rivals Burslem, a team whose attack was spearheaded by West Indian Tom Dewdney, who was, according to David, 'the first really quick bowler I faced.' After dismissing their opponents for 82, Newcastle were struggling at 24 for four when nephew was joined by uncle. Stan quickly weighed up the situation. 'You have Dewdney until I get my eye in,' he instructed. David obliged, the runs came, and the game was won. The championship success proved a fitting end to his tenure at Newcastle.

David had earned recognition by the Staffordshire selectors as early as 1958. However, his debut, against Cheshire at Oxendon, brought frustration when he was run out without scoring. This fact may provide solace for some of his subsequent 'victims'. His batting partner on this occasion was Jack Ikin, formerly of Lancashire and England. Ikin, a Staffordshire man, was born and died in Bignall End. He first came to the notice of Lancashire when he represented Staffordshire against the red rose Second XI and caught the scout's eye with his confident handling of paceman Eddie Phillipson. Ikin played in eighteen Test matches, the most memorable of which was the third Test against South Africa at Old Trafford in 1951. Opening the batting with Len Hutton in the second innings against a hostile and ferocious attack spearheaded by the fair-haired Cuan McCarthy on a rain-damaged pitch, his 38 runs proved crucial in England's nine-wicket victory. Asked if he thought his partner had played well, Hutton, who had watched Ikin's brave but punishing innings, replied, 'Yes, but he didn't play him like a great batsman, did he? A great batsman would have been down the other end.' Which, of course, Hutton was.

Jack Ikin, an early influence on David's cricket career.

Ikin retired from the first-class game in 1957 and returned to Staffordshire where he captained the county side for a further ten years. As David became an established member of the team, his admiration of his captain grew. Many of Ikin's qualities – balance, quickness on his feet and gutsy determination – became features of his own game. Playing at Wolverhampton against Bedfordshire, David saw him score a hundred before lunch in impeccable style.

'I enjoyed that,' Ikin remarked, leaning on the pavilion veranda during the interval.

'I enjoyed watching it,' his protégé replied.

1962 was David's last season with his native county. He batted at number three, sharing the distinction with Ikin and David Hancock of scoring over 600 runs during the Minor Counties campaign. During that summer his achievements were noted by Ken Turner, secretary at Northamptonshire and ever alert to talent emerging in

Minor Counties cricket. He discussed his interest with Brian Crump: 'Who's this chap Steele at Staffordshire?'

'He's my cousin.'

'Well, you better get him here then.'

The die was almost cast.

However, there was competition from a quarter nearer to home. His friend and former Staffordshire teammate, wicketkeeper Bob Taylor, had joined Derbyshire and mentioned David to his coach, Denis Smith. Denis watched him in action and gave him a call.

'I like the look of you. Come for a trial.'

David confessed that he had no transport. Smith responded in characteristically sardonic fashion.

'Have you got a bike? It's only thirty miles or so. Start early.'

The trial took place one Saturday morning in the dilapidated 'aviary' that passed for an indoor school. Early in his knock, David received a ball that 'went through the pad' causing intense pain. The

Staffordshire in 1962, David's final year with the minor county.
Back: Peter Gibbs, Frank Colclough, Jim Pedley, Brian Tatton, Ben
Griffiths, Brian James. Front: Ivan Frost, David Steele, Jack Ikin,
Harold Boon, David Hancock.

bowler was none other than Les Jackson, the England Test player who amassed a total of 1,730 wickets in his long career. Only one bowler, in David's experience, was capable of inflicting similar discomfort – Somerset's Fred Rumsey.

It was of little consequence, however, as David was already committed to Northampton and it would be seventeen years before he joined Denis Smith at Derby.

Transport had been a recurring problem for some time and, with journeys to and from cricketing venues becoming increasingly difficult, it became vital for David to learn to drive. He began instruction in 1962 when his first tutor, old school friend Keith Snape, an electrician down the mines and father of England spinner Jeremy, introduced him to clutch control, gear-changing and other mysteries of life behind the wheel. He proved a slow learner, failing his driving test on two occasions, but early in 1963 decided to back his fragile confidence by purchasing a car of his own. By then the money he had been saving from his stipend at Newcastle CC had reached the not-inconsiderable sum of £350. When his father heard of his plans he arranged the construction of a garage at the side of the house.

As the footings were being dug, a curious neighbour asked Alf, 'Are you having a car then?'

David's father replied, in typically blunt fashion: 'The only car we've got in this house is a Dinky.'

Early in 1963, Keith took David to the Hanley Motor Mart to make the purchase. He was quickly seduced by a cream Morris 1000 complete with leopard-skin seats and 12,000 miles on the clock. The asking price of £475 was less attractive. After failing to negotiate an improved deal, David was forced to leave the sale room empty handed. Returning home he confronted his father, who sat, reading a newspaper and smoking his pipe, in his familiar armchair.

'How did you get on then?' Alf asked, barely raising his eyes above the paper.

'Saw the car. But I'm £125 short,' David replied.

His father's initial response was unsympathetic. 'Well you'll have to earn it, then,' he said, returning to the sports pages. Perhaps sens-

The infamous Morris 1000, a car cursed by many a Steele passenger.

ing David's disappointment, Alf relented, slightly. 'I'll lend you the rest of the money. Pay me back in September.' Then, 'Mother, go upstairs to the little blue bag and bring me £125.'

Keith and David returned to the showroom, travelling on Turner's bus, and discovered to their relief that 'the little beauty was still there – and we did the deal.'

Now the proud owner of a car and accompanied by Keith Snape and Alf, David presented himself for his third driving test in April 1963. After dropping off his two passengers he completed the circuit and returned to the test centre where his father was awaiting the outcome. It was soon apparent.

'Take the L plates off the front, I'll do the back,' David instructed, and prepared to drive home. But on arriving at 134 High Lane the novice driver indicated to turn into the driveway, failed to judge the width of the gateway and crushed the semaphore indicator against the gate post.

It was a minor setback. His apprenticeships were over. He'd completed his indentures at the Wedgwood Press, passed his driving test and was a league cricketer no more. On the morning of Monday 5 April 1963, he turned his car out of the drive and headed south.

He was Northampton-bound.

PART TWO

BLOCKING, SCORING, TRAPPING, HIGHLIGHTING

4

MAKING A MARK

According to the author and political activist Tariq Ali, the bohemian style in Oxford in 1963 – the year he went up to Exeter College – was black plastic or leather jackets for women and black leather or navy donkey jackets for men. He admits to sticking with 'cavalry twills and a duffle coat, at least for a few months'. It's unlikely there were too many bohemians present in The Parks on 8 June of that year as Oxford University hosted Northamptonshire a few weeks before the Varsity Match at Lord's, but this was David's debut in first-class cricket. Batsman Roy Wills and seam bowler John Davis were also making their first appearances, and in the case of Davis, a seam bowler from Cheshire, his last as well. Wills, in contrast, played thirty-three matches over seven seasons but extended his involvement with the club as Second XI captain, co-founder of the reformed county colts side, committee member (chairing the hiring-and-firing cricket sub-committee but stepping down when his son-in-law Rob Bailey became captain) and – most recently – matchday host to officials from visiting counties. But would the rune-readers have been able to spot a future BBC Sports Personality of the Year in the county's side? Brought into the attack by acting-captain Roger Prideaux (regular skipper Keith Andrew was with England in the first Test against Frank Worrell's West Indians at Old Trafford) as third change, he

Glasses and a hint of grey: it was in his last year at Endon Secondary Modern that David was diagnosed with poor eyesight. When he arrived at Northamptonshire in 1963, his glasses combined with prematurely greying hair to give early notice of his trademark features.

opened his account of first-class victims by having the Nawab of Pataudi caught at square leg by Peter Watts, brother of Jim, for 33: 'Not a brilliant delivery, but it was there.' He also removed Maurice Manasseh and wicketkeeper Andrew Mason to finish with the perfectly respectable figures of three for 65 from twenty-four overs. What would become a fixed-factor in his Northamptonshire career also began in this innings; cousin Brian Crump asked if he could have David at leg slip. He would remain there for much of the next decade. Batting at number six, he had time to score ten unbeaten runs – and see Prideaux through to a double-century – before the declaration came. His abiding memory of the match would be the imposing presence and athleticism of 'Tiger' Pataudi, already India's captain at the age of twenty-two, chasing a ball to the boundary and – unable to pull up in time – vaulting one of the benches surrounding the ground.

Brian Reynolds, senior pro and Kettering neighbour to the young David Steele.

The 1963 season was a momentous one in the English game. It saw the start of the first fully fledged limited-overs competition, soon to be become the Gillette Cup, and was the first in which everyone playing at county level was a 'cricketer' rather than an amateur or a professional. The distinction, and with it the traditional Gentlemen versus Players fixtures, had been abolished the previous winter. Prideaux (Tonbridge School and Cambridge University) appeared in the last G-v-P at Lord's in July 1962, having joined Northamptonshire from Kent as Assistant Secretary – a popular device to allow those who wanted amateur status to achieve and retain it. A future England batsman, Prideaux was also appointed Andrew's vice-captain and would eventually succeed him. David wasn't too fussed about this watershed moment in sporting and social history, any more than he would have paid heed to what the poet Phillip Larkin reckoned 1963 marked the start of. He had his professional contract – initially three years at £400 per annum – and set about the task of making himself into a county cricketer.

One of the first rites of passage to be observed was finding digs. After a false start – his mother ran a finger over the furniture and inspected the dust with ill-concealed disgust, prompting David's observation that 'you're not in Stoke now, Mum' – he ended up with Ma Dickens in Manfield Road, one of the streets of red-brick Victorian terraced houses near the County Ground which, years later, prompted *Daily Telegraph* reporter Doug Ibbotson to describe Northamptonshire's headquarters as 'Coronation Street with grass'. The gaze of the stuffed animals in their glass cases could be slightly disconcerting at times, but Ma looked after her lodgers well and David was soon joined there by teammate Mike Kettle, the left-arm seamer from Stamford. Northampton's social delights in those days included Wednesday night dances at The Salon, where Errol Flynn had been a regular during his spell with the town's Repertory Company in the 1930s. It was there that David met a girl from the village of Weldon near Corby, the start of the most important partnership in his life.

David's first match in Northamptonshire colours was in early May 1963, a Second XI fixture against Nottinghamshire at Wantage Road under the captaincy of Dennis Brookes. The quietly spoken Yorkshireman devoted his entire adult life to the club, aside from service in the Second World War, joining the playing staff as a teenager in the early 1930s (helped, he claimed modestly, by his ability to type and thus help out in the office), progressing to senior professional, captain, coach and manager of the new indoor school, assistant secretary and eventually president. His house backed on to the ground at Northampton, and he continued to do his daily lap – latterly with the aid of a walking frame – until shortly before his death aged ninety in 2006. When Mister Brookes spoke people listened, from Test players downwards, and within a few days of hitting 120 not out for the 'stiffs' against Warwickshire at Corby, David found himself walking out with the first team at Oxford. He was picked again against the touring Pakistan Eaglets at Peterborough and was able to watch Mushtaq Mohammad – with whom he would probably spend more time at the batting crease than anyone else during his career – hit a second-innings century. By the end of the summer, Northampton-shire had signed *him* too.

It was also appropriate in a way that his maiden County Champi-onship innings, against Lancashire at Old Trafford on 4 July, should be ended by a fellow Staffordshire man. Ken Higgs bowled him for 16; David promptly returned the compliment when the hosts batted! He stayed in Northamptonshire's side for the remainder of the season without achieving much of note, but more of him was seen in 1964: nineteen matches, 773 runs, twenty-seven wickets (including that of Tom Graveney after the supreme stylist had scored the hundredth century of his career at Worcester, of which more anon) and twenty catches. The county finished third in the table, behind Worcestershire and Warwickshire, and at the AGM in March 1965 club president 'Tubby' Vials (who had captained the side to the runners-up spot way back in 1912) insisted the current team 'could not be very far away from the Championship'.

It is hard for Northamptonshire supporters of a certain vintage to contemplate the 1965 season's denouement without putting a se-vere strain on the blood pressure monitoring equipment. And, no, Hampshire's buccaneering skipper Colin Ingleby-Mackenzie has still not been forgiven. The basic facts are that Keith Andrew's men start-ed poorly – bottom of the table at the end of May – but then some-thing clicked and they proceeded to win thirteen matches, leading the Championship from mid-July until Worcestershire pipped them at the post. Don Kenyon's side had received an unexpected leg-up to the title in their penultimate match at Bournemouth when Ingers, ever the gambler, declared 146 behind to make a game of it, and Hampshire were promptly skittled for 31 in their second innings. Worcestershire then beat Sussex along the south coast at Hove and retained the pennant by four points.

It was a memorable if pretty damp campaign, made special for David by the award of his Northamptonshire cap in June. This was, after all, the very best kind of recognition for a professional crick-eter, involving both prestige within the side and a few extra bob. He

Keith Andrew, the wicketkeeper-captain who so-nearly led Northamptonshire to the title in 1965.

passed 1,000 first-class runs in a season for the first time and held forty catches, just three behind Colin Milburn's county record set the previous year and fourth in the country among non-wicketkeepers. He even warranted a brief name-check in a magazine article on Northamptonshire's near-miss penned by the great Neville Cardus: '[Keith] Andrew has stirred the best out of the talents of his colleagues, the violent swashbuckling Milburn, the versatile Wattses, the dependable Prideaux, the long-limbed Larter, the insidious seamer Crump, the worthy serviceable Reynolds, the attractively useful fair-haired Norman – not forgetting Scott, Steele, Bailey, Sully, Wills and all.' It's questionable whether the soon-to-be Sir Neville had seen much of David in action at that stage and he died a few months before the stirring events of 1975. But the inference of the piece – that this was a team greater than the sum of its parts – was entirely accurate.

'Ollie' Milburn was the star, of course. His innings of 152 not out against Gloucestershire in the final fixture at Wantage Road was arguably his greatest for the county. Made in under two sessions, it included seven sixes and fifteen fours and kept alive hopes of victory in a match cut short by rain which Northamptonshire needed to win to keep Worcestershire at arm's length. David came to relish the sight of the 'builder's backside' belonging to the big lad from Burnopfield heading out to the middle, for two main reasons. A batting exhibition of stunning power and virtuosity could follow, and more mundanely it freed up a bit of room in the pokey changing facilities at Northampton. 'Ollie had six pegs and kit everywhere,' David recalled. 'Off the field he dressed immaculately and spent a fortune on clothes, but in the dressing room he wasn't the tidiest.' In another corner would sit senior pro Brian Reynolds – neat, organised and self-disciplined. All the things Ollie wasn't. But this knock against Gloucestershire, with the groundstaff hovering ready to transform the place from county cricket venue to First Division football stadium (the 1965-66 season would be Northampton Town's only in the top flight), was special. It deserved to win a Championship but the rain returned and it didn't.

A couple of weeks earlier, Northamptonshire believed they had taken a big step towards that elusive first title when they overcame fellow contenders Glamorgan at the Arms Park in Cardiff. This wasn't cricket for the Twenty20 generation, it was trench warfare, and the Staffordshire cousins relished every hard-fought minute. David's 55 in the first innings was the joint-highest individual score of the game, while Crump sent down 76.2 overs for match figures of eight for 132 and was carried off the field when Northamptonshire won by 18 runs – without the services of their England fast bowler, the towering David Larter, on international duty against South Africa. Andrew and Larter were the only current Test players in the county's team that season. Milburn made his debut the following summer, Prideaux a couple of years after that, and David later still.

If Brutus was right and 'there is a tide in the affairs of men which taken at the flood leads on the fortune,' Northamptonshire had missed it. In 1966, David again topped 1,000 runs and also had the satisfaction of securing his best bowling figures in first-class cricket, eight for 29 against Lancashire at Northampton. He always felt Andrew was reluctant to bowl him, hence his determination to make the most of any opportunity that presented itself. Fellow spinners Haydn Sully and Malcolm Scott did most of the work in the first innings, but the visitors were building a handy lead through openers David Green – later a popular addition to the cricket press corps – and Geoff Pullar in their second dig before David broke through. He added two more wickets before the close, Lancashire finishing the day four down, and claims he almost had to grab the ball from the captain next morning to keep himself on. On this occasion, David proved his point, bowling 'with venom' to do so. He never got a sniff of a single over, though, at Cardiff (not the Arms Park this time but the new ground at Sophia Gardens) in 1967 when Crump and Bedford-born seamer Ray Bailey bowled unchanged throughout both innings. It was another triumph for the family, however, as David and Brian shared a crucial 62-run partnership in a low-scoring

Northamptonshire in 1966.
Back: Jack Mercer (scorer), Mushtaq Mohammad, David Steele, Ray Bailey, Malcolm Scott, Haydn Sully, Colin Milburn, Jack Jennings (physio). Front: Brian Crump, Roger Prideaux, Keith Andrew, Brian Reynolds, Jim Watts.

match, another instance of Crump more than earning his traditional post-match drink of choice, a pint of milk.

Green, incidentally, used to tell the story of David staying put and re-marking his guard one day at Old Trafford when the rest of the Lancashire side were convinced Ken Higgs had found the edge. So incensed was the fellow Staffordshire man that when it came to catching the train from Manchester to Stoke – where Higgs, Steele and Crump were all staying – he declined not only to share a compartment with the batsman who had 'done him' but wouldn't even get on the same train, preferring to remain on the platform.

By 1967, Keith Andrew had retired. Sharing a fate later endured by Bob Taylor – widely regarded as the best wicketkeeper in England but not scoring enough runs to please the Test selectors – he ranks as one of Northamptonshire's most successful captains of all time, leading the side to third, second and fifth place in the table in his last three summers in charge. He also followed an entirely personal path. David called him 'Walter' after Walter Mitty, while fellow Lancastrian Frank

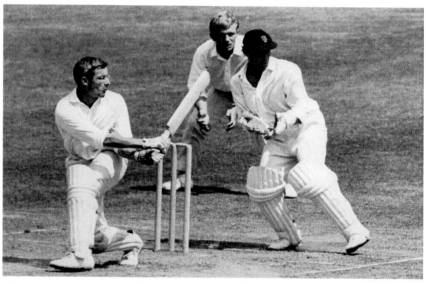

Sweeping Middlesex's Peter Parfitt in July 1967. Clive Radley fields at slip with Mike Sturt behind the stumps.

Roger Prideaux, David's county captain for four seasons between 1967 and 1970.

Tyson described him as 'absent-minded to the degree that he often forgot what he was saying in mid-sentence… and would frequently wander off into cloud-cuckoo land.' Ken Turner once spotted Andrew reading *Wisden* in the gents toilet to gen up on the opposition's strengths and weaknesses before taking the field. But whatever he did and however he did it, it seemed to work. His successor as captain, Roger Prideaux, fared less well.

The batting statistics mark Prideaux out as one of Northamptonshire's best ever, and David was full of admiration for his unselfishness as Milburn's opening partner – usually giving Ollie as much of the bowling as possible. Against Essex at Clacton in 1966, Milburn took out his frustration after being dropped by England and smashed 203 out of 293 in a shade over four hours, Prideaux giving him full rein before taking over the assault himself once the big man had gone and finishing 153 not out. Coming in at tea-time, Milburn pronounced himself 'knackered' and David remembers wishing he could act like a human petrol station, pumping extra energy into this huge, perspiring frame – which promptly got out more-or-less immediately. In one of those little quirks that delight cricket nerds, both openers were then out for a duck in the second innings, leaving David and Mushtaq to finish the job and secure victory.

Prideaux was a strong man capable of savaging bowlers, especially one or two pacemen around the circuit he didn't much care for, and had a pleasing line in dry humour. Once, finding himself being comprehensively outscored by David, he enquired of his junior partner: 'Steeley, are you on drugs?' As this wasn't a particularly common occurrence it's possible a few of the spectators were thinking along similar lines. He was, like Andrew, an individual, but didn't possess his predecessor's whimsical nature – as David said, 'he was a top-notch player and I absolutely loved his cricket. But I probably wouldn't have gone on holiday with him.' Sometimes Prideaux had every reason to feel a tad exasperated with his side. Against Derbyshire at Ilkeston in 1969, Northamptonshire were a long way adrift on first innings and

David and wife Carol share a joke with the much-missed Colin Milburn.

the skipper instructed a cautious approach. Instead, Fred Goldstein, the hard-hitting Rhodes scholar who captained Oxford University, set off like a train. Mushtaq and Albert Lightfoot joined in the fun, and with Prideaux himself reaching three figures he ended up declaring and having Derbyshire seven wickets down when time ran out. 'When I tell you to smash it, you block it – and when I tell you to block it...'

Under Prideaux, David's regular batting position was number five in the role of 'stabiliser', useful with the likes of Milburn and Mushtaq in the side. He found it difficult to relax on the field and admitted later that his intensity sometimes held him back, even manifesting itself physically when he grew particularly tense. One day, fighting hard against Somerset, he found his breakfast returning. When David got out, Jim Watts was allegedly less than delighted at having to take his guard on a piece of this morning's hotel bacon. In his England days, David spoke of 'wanting to try until it hurts', a concept his Northamptonshire teammates were only too familiar with.

The 1969 season brought a fresh challenge with the advent of the John Player League. On paper, Northamptonshire looked better equipped than most with one of the circuit's most miserly bowlers in Crump – so tight he 'wouldn't give you the dirt from under his fingernails' – and some attractive stroke-makers including Mushtaq, the young Peter Willey, South African Hylton Ackerman and his regular drinking partner Milburn. In the county's second home match in the competition, against Worcestershire, *Wisden* records that 'Milburn had to retire through illness' – a scene reminiscent of David's own gastric indiscretion, although the cause reputedly owed less to pent-up tension than a big Saturday night out. A fortnight later, Northamptonshire were playing Middlesex at Lord's in the JPL without Ollie. Travelling home from a party after the county's match against the West Indian tourists, the car carrying Milburn plus teammates George Sharp and Dennis Breakwell collided with a lorry. The England batsman's face hit the windscreen and surgeons later had to remove his left eye. It was a tragedy for his county, his country and the game as a whole, but even more so for Milburn himself. Although he returned to county cricket a few years later – once retrieving his glass eye from the middle of the pitch whilst bowling, and cleaning it in his mouth – this superb sporting entertainer struggled to find direction and happiness in his life thereafter. He died of a heart attack in 1990 aged only forty-eight, and his story was later told in the play *When the Eye Has Gone* by James Graham-Brown. Few of his old teammates can talk about Ollie without raw emotion kicking in, and certainly not David: 'Colin was "instant" in everything he did, so natural, like when he hit [Hampshire fast bowler] Butch White on the up over cover, taking tiles off the signal box roof. I never walk past there now without thinking of that shot. Viv Richards is the nearest I've seen to his genius.'

Within a few weeks of Milburn's accident, David found himself ruled out for the season after having his arm broken by Mike Procter. He returned to the fray in 1970, a summer that saw both David and Northamptonshire marking time. One major plus for the county was the return to the first-class game of Jim Watts. He had left it in 1966 to pursue a business career, unwilling to become, in his words, 'a no-hoper who's sacked at thirty.' When Prideaux called it a day at Wantage Road and moved to Sussex, Watts was appointed captain for 1971. For David, the road to greater things was about to open up.

5

ON THE UP

Like politics, county cricket can be a thoroughly ruthless business. Anything that involves a large number of aspirants looking to fill a small and finite number of spaces, whether in a sports team or the House of Commons, is bound to arouse jealousy and rivalry. Tony Benn revealed in his diaries that he didn't wish to make public a serious illness he was being treated for because the political parties would instantly look up his majority and consider who should contest the by-election. At Northamptonshire, the top order was always going to look very different in 1971 in the wake of Milburn's accident, Reynolds' release from the staff, Albert Lightfoot's retirement, Prideaux's county switch and Goldstein's return to southern Africa. David had been the stabiliser at number five under Andrew and Prideaux; Watts moved him up the order to perform a similar role at number three. Not immediately, though. He began the season in his accustomed position as the new skipper attempted to mould his side, a task rendered that much trickier by the absence of Mushtaq on international duty for some matches in the first half of the season and problems with identifying a regular opening pair; no fewer than eight players went in first during the summer. To their credit, the committee wanted young cricketers to be (according to the top table at the Annual Meeting in March) 'thrown in at the deep end'. This far-sighted

*Cousin Crump in action:
Brian claimed 807 wickets
for Northamptonshire.*

policy's most conspicuous success was the emergence of Geoff Cook, who scored his maiden century. It also placed more responsibility on the shoulders of senior players like David.

The key match for him came at the end of June when Lancashire visited Wantage Road. Promoted to three, behind openers Peter Willey and Hylton Ackerman, he made 118, adding 222 for the third wicket with Mushtaq. He had found his new niche, or perhaps his new-old one, returning to his preferred position from Staffordshire days. Watts also reached three figures in an exciting match of three declarations that Northamptonshire lost off the first ball of the final over. Next day, the side moved on to Worcester, and in another game dominated by the bat David notched an unbeaten 140, the highest score of his 500-match first-class career. For a batsman with the reputation of relishing the occupation of the crease, it's a relatively modest personal best. David's sons both quizzed him about it in later

Mushtaq Mohammad, the Pakistan all-rounder who shared twelve years in the Northamptonshire team with David.

years and the best he could do by way of explanation was to quote (or possibly misquote) The Master, Sir Jack Hobbs, who supposedly claimed that 'a hundred will do'. Unfortunately, the statistics show that Hobbs exceeded 140 on sixty-four occasions, including fifteen 'doubles' and a 'treble'.

David finished 1971 with 1,444 runs and thirty-one wickets in the Championship, second in both sets of averages for Northamptonshire behind Watts and Willey respectively. 'The main batting honours went to Steele, who improved on previous form and looked an accomplished player,' noted *Wisden*'s long-serving Wantage Road correspondent Fred Speakman. 'His bowling was very useful and he took many brilliant catches.' The committee authorised a £100 bonus for his performances as well as making him vice-captain, Crump retaining the title (and payment) as 'senior cricketer' to avoid any family embarrassment. But Speakman (a much-loved figure around the County Ground, 'rumpled but never ruffled' according to Matthew Engel) also flagged up the need for bowling reinforcements, a priority made even more pressing as Sarfraz Nawaz, the Pakistani paceman recommended to the club by Prideaux following MCC's tour there in 1968-69, failed to make his mark and was released. He would, of course, be back, but Ken Turner was intent on addressing the problem; by November he was reporting back on his conversations and manoeuvres. Bob Willis wasn't interested and he ended up moving from Surrey to Warwickshire. However, Bob Cottam agreed a move from Hampshire and John 'Doc' Dye came from Kent. They would form a new-ball pairing the envy of most other counties, right-arm and left-arm, even if they didn't always see eye to eye, especially when it came to their fielding off each other's bowling: 'You're not exactly Alberto Juantorena yourself, are you?' And there was another significant signing with the beguiling Indian left-arm spinner Bishan Bedi, a tormentor of England's batsmen in 1971, also heading to Northampton. The arrival of 'Bish' spelled the beginning of one of David's most enduring cricket friendships, even if it greatly reduced his own bowling opportunities. And no one could deny that the acquisition of Cottam, Dye and Bedi represented an outstanding bit of business on the club's part – the trio claimed 1,016 wickets for Northamptonshire between 1972 and 1977. Watts would later insist, surely correctly, that a team comprising the bowling attack of '72 and the batting line-up of '80 (Geoff Cook, Wayne Larkins, Richard Williams, Allan Lamb and Peter Willey) would have won the County Championship at a canter.

In fact, the new-look strike force didn't operate together until June of that Ashes summer after the county's efforts to secure a special registration for Cottam failed. He took out his frustration on Oxford University at The Parks – figures of eight for 14 to complement a Steele century – before getting down to business in earnest. Among David's many significant performances during a campaign which saw Northamptonshire climb from fourteenth place to fourth in the Championship was a memorable game against Surrey at Northampton at the end of June. Early in his first innings, a ball from Robin

John Dye: part of a new bowling attack that led Northamptonshire into the 1970s.

Jackman reared up and caught him a nasty blow on the ear. He left the field, had the wound inspected by physio Jack Jennings, and was taken to Northampton General Hospital where the deep cut was stitched. When he returned to the ground he discovered that the team was struggling, already six wickets down, and that he was needed to bat. It proved a short stay at the wicket as he top-edged a bouncer from the unsympathetic Jackman and was brilliantly caught at deep-square leg by substitute fielder, Dudley Owen-Thomas for 15. If the first innings had been underwhelming for both David and the team, dismissed for 134, the second was something of a triumph. A partnership of 234 with Mushtaq saw both players score centuries, their defiant efforts preventing defeat. David put the pain behind him, continually playing forward to Jackman who became increasingly frustrated at the batsman's obduracy. At last the bowler stopped his run-up to enquire if his adversary knew that he had two studs missing from his front boot.

'What about the back foot?' David replied.

'I never see that,' a disgruntled Jackman muttered.

The Steele-Mushtaq combination also contributed to a first-ever victory over the Australians in August. If the likes of Ian Chappell and Dennis Lillee treated David like a faintly bizarre interloper when he made his Test debut against them three years later, it suggests either deficient memories or (more likely) a total lack of interest in run-of-the-mill matches against English counties. The elder Chappell brought his side to Wantage Road having lost the Ashes with defeat on a controversial pitch at Headingley, but with an opportunity to level the series in the final match at The Oval. If that was their focus – above a tussle with Northamptonshire – it's hard to blame them, although they subsequently copped some flak from their own press for their apparently cavalier attitude. The Sydney *Sun* called it 'a circus' but Ken Turner observed pithily that 'the better team won'. The tourists were dismissed for 191 by Bedi and Willey, and Watts'

Jim Watts looks on as Northamptonshire pick up a cheque for beating the Australians in 1972.

men looked set for a sizeable lead before collapsing from 142 for two to 210 all out, Mushtaq running out of partners on 88. Then Bedi wove his spell again, adding four wickets to his five in the first innings, which left Northamptonshire requiring only 125 to win in a full day's play. With Bob Massie, surprise hero of the Lord's Test that summer, unfit to bowl, it was hardly a challenging target. When Lillee removed Mushtaq with only 22 more needed, Watts sent in Crump – in his benefit year – to join cousin David. A family affair to delight the sentimental? Not exactly. With just a single to his name, the popular beneficiary was run out by a distance. 'We didn't know Bruce Francis had a throw like a bullet,' recalled David. 'He was fielding in front of the West Stand and in it came like a tracer. Brian didn't get halfway.' It was left to Steele and Watts to tidy up, Northamptonshire winning by seven wickets just before lunch with Steele unbeaten on 60. Remember the name, Dennis.

There were those who would have handed David an Ashes debut in Ray Illingworth's side that season. The *Evening Standard*'s cricket correspondent, John Thicknesse, flagged up his propensity for playing straight, 'and there aren't so many Englishmen you can say that about.' He suggested David might have stood more of a chance had he played his cricket at a more fashionable county than Northamptonshire. Perish the thought.

Crump played only two more first-class matches – against Middlesex and Somerset – before his career with the club ended. At the contracts meeting a few days after the win over Australia, the committee decided not to re-engage Crump at the age of thirty-four. By 1972 he was playing largely as a batsman and, after volunteering to open the innings, made a battling unbeaten century against Derbyshire at Chesterfield in July. But it wasn't enough as the club looked to cut the size of the professional staff to free up funds for additional recruitment. A pay out of £4,000 from his benefit may not have been much of a consolation for Stan's lad, especially after a career which saw him send down over 54,000 deliveries for Northamptonshire, collecting 807 wickets, the sixth-highest tally in the club's history. Possessing neither searing pace nor prodigious spin, his unspectacular cricketing craftsmanship was a key feature in the county's rise from also-rans to serious Championship contenders.

The revolving door turned again. Out went Crump and Laurie Johnson, talented and humorous understudy to Keith Andrew for so many seasons and latterly displaced behind the stumps by George Sharp. In came the reliable opening batsman and slip-catcher Roy Virgin from Somerset. Sarfraz, after impressing for the Second XI during 1973 as he honed his craft for Nelson in the Lancashire League, returned to the staff for the following season, when he also toured England with Pakistan and appeared in all three Tests. Northamptonshire's professional staff may have been relatively small (only fifteen players were used in the Championship in 1973) but it made up for in quality what it lacked in quantity. And Turner's shrewdness, both in finance and recruiting, was a major factor.

Turner had run a highly lucrative football pool competition in the 1950s which, at its peak, boasted 80,000 members paying a shilling a week. It helped to fund the first indoor cricket school at Wantage Road – the building that now bears Turner's name – but, like most schemes of its kind, eventually reached its sell-by (or buy-by) date. In 1969 Northamptonshire made a loss for the first time in seventeen years; retrenchment measures included scrapping the county colts side and taking a long, hard look at the club's long-established policy of using outgrounds. Kettering and Peterborough followed Rushden in losing their county fixtures. But the ingenuity of KCT manifested itself again as he reinvented himself as an unlikely pop music impresario, staging first discos and then rock concerts at the County Ground, to the dismay of local residents. The prediction of a senior police officer that 'there will be trouble, Ken' certainly came true, but hundreds turned up to hear the likes of Suzi Quatro, Siouxsie and the Banshees and Leo Sayer (Turner also booked the Sex Pistols but they failed to show), and notwithstanding an occasional court appearance the club's coffers received a welcome boost.

Back in 1967, Northamptonshire's first sponsored car, a Ford Cortina, had driven out of the gates at Wantage Road with skipper Roger Prideaux at the helm and Albert Lightfoot in the passenger seat, bound for Trent Bridge and a Championship fixture with Nottinghamshire. It heralded a return to post-war days when players used their own vehicles to travel to matches. By the early seventies, David, one of the few owners of a car amongst the players, had become a designated driver, carrying three teammates, the shove ha'penny board and the first aid kit in his little red Mini, also known as the little red ambulance. His usual fellow travellers from those days, young prospects Alan Tait, Wayne Larkins and Geoff Cook, will no doubt recall the journeys with mixed feelings. David's driving may have improved since his early experiences in the Morris 1000 but navigation was at its most rudimentary, satnav was years away, the AA map book rarely accessed and fundamental questions, such as 'which way to Cardiff?' answered with a stock response: 'If in doubt, head south.'

Variations in the Northamptonshire line up meant occasional changes to the occupants of David's car. Another youngster from the north, Yorkshireman Norman Maltby, made little impact on the cricket field during his brief spell at Wantage Road, but enjoyed a fleeting moment in the limelight when travelling back to Northampton from Chelmsford and a Championship match against Essex in the tiny vehicle. David's scores of 68 and 46 had contributed to a handsome Northamptonshire victory, clinched by Bishan Bedi's second innings haul of seven for 34, but the day's exertions took their toll on the drive home. With space at a premium in the tiny vehicle David's legs began to stiffen and he was suddenly gripped by excruciating cramps. He had little alternative but to stop the car, get out and lay on the grass verge alongside the road in an attempt to ease the pain. After several minutes spent gingerly massaging his calves he heard the engine suddenly spark into life and looked up to see the vehicle beginning to move off. Struggling to his feet, he hobbled after the car which, he noticed, had Norman Maltby at the wheel. When it eventually came to a stop and the laughter within began to subside, David addressed the young driver.

'You took off beautifully,' he said. 'I didn't know you could drive.'

'I've had three lessons,' Maltby confessed, sheepishly.

'Well,' came the reply, 'you'd better carry on then. Just go easy on the clutch.'

The journey continued without further incident and, on their arrival at the County Ground, David presented the surrogate driver with a mock driving licence recording his feat. Sadly for Maltby he had no opportunity to repeat the experience. It proved to be his only appearance in a Championship match away from Wantage Road.

Passengers in the little red Mini were discomforted further by the driver's insistence, born of his thrifty nature, that the car was capable of achieving seventy miles to the gallon when in reality it was nearer to forty-five, with inevitable repercussions. A notable victim of David's misplaced faith in the Mini's fuel economy was Mushtaq, who had unwisely secured a lift back to Northampton after a game. When the car ran out of petrol on the journey home – not once, but twice – he declaimed that he would never travel with Steele again. Some weeks later David and roommate Jim Watts had settled down to sleep in the team hotel in Weston-Super-Mare when he received a phone call from Mushtaq.

'Hello Daddy,' the Pakistani began, using his usual method of addressing his near-contemporary. 'I've broken down in Bristol, Willey and Cottam have abandoned me, I'm so cold, can you come and pick me up?'

David turned to his captain, who lay, only dark eyebrows visible above the bedclothes.

'Jim – Mushie's broken down. He wants us to go and rescue him.' Watts was unmoved. 'Sorry, Mush, Jim's not interested. Get a lift!'

'You t***, Steeley!' an aggrieved Mushtaq began but was quickly cut short.

'Mo. I clearly recall you announcing to the world just a couple of weeks ago that you would never travel in my car again. Say sorry, and I'll try Jim again.' A muttered apology followed. 'Skipper, your best player is stranded in Bristol. Are we going to collect him or not?'

Still buried beneath the sheets, Watts remained silent for several seconds before lifting his head and nodding begrudgingly. They dressed and set off to locate Mushtaq but had hardly left the hotel car park before Jim motioned towards the dashboard.

'What's that red light mean?' he asked.

The driver was all too familiar with the warning. 'We're running out of petrol,' he replied.

Fortunately they found a garage, put in David's customary five pound's worth of fuel and set off to find their stranded teammate. Mission accomplished.

On the pitch, Watts' tactical nous and wry sense of humour, plus his uncanny knack of predicting the weather ('if he pitched up wearing a raincoat we'd know rain would stop play later' as David recalled), welded a group of talented individuals into a team to be reckoned with. And in 1973 Bedi was his trump card, becoming the first bowler since Haydn Sully seven years earlier to take 100 first-class wickets in a season for Northamptonshire. In alien conditions it was a truly remarkable achievement, not repeated until another Indian spinner, Anil Kumble, took the county scene by storm in 1995. There was, though, a knock-on effect for David, who was

A study in concentration.

given only twenty-one Championship overs compared to Bedi's 695. This wouldn't have surprised or perturbed Bishan who, years later, explained to his biographer, Suresh Menon, his decision to join this particular county: 'It wasn't one of the fashionable clubs. The ground was poor, the facilities were lousy. They were looking for a left-arm spinner, and it just happened that way.' On his first day in the nets, he said, 'a whole bunch were bowling left-arm spin – David Steele and George Sharp among them. One was a batsman and the other the wicketkeeper. This team really needed a left-arm spinner!'

The batsman label didn't take account of David's 200-odd wickets for the club before Bedi arrived, but there was no jealousy on the part of the established professional. David knew a class act when he saw one, although he believed Bedi was expected to bowl too many overs for Northamptonshire which, taken along with his heavy international commitments during the winter, cost him his 'bounce' after five years on the county circuit. But he described fielding around the corner to Bedi as one of the most enjoyable experiences of his long career, marvelling at the dip, loop, spin and variation of the Indian master, who was known occasionally to applaud a batsman who clouted him for six – all part of the master plan. For the record, there are no recorded instances of David emulating this gesture.

Watts' side moved up one place to third in 1973 with David (picked for MCC against the touring New Zealanders at Lord's in May but caught behind off Richard Collinge for a duck as the match squelched to a soggy draw) logging 1,213 Championship runs including three centuries. Mushtaq also reached four figures and the pace pair, Cottam and Dye, shared 122 wickets. Bizarrely, one committee man berated Watts for 'lack of leadership' during the season, notably in the limited-overs games, and bemoaned 'the failure to win anything'. A harsh judgement, but it's worth pointing out that Northamptonshire were indeed pretty clueless in the 40-over competition until the following season when they surprised everyone, including possibly themselves, by winning ten matches and finishing fourth in the John Player. Personally, 1974 wasn't a vintage year for David, although it started well enough as he held a low slip catch to

remove Geoffrey Boycott off the bowling of Sarfraz in the early moments of the opening three-day fixture against Yorkshire at Wantage
Road. Not surprisingly, perhaps, Boycott was one of David's favourite players throughout their respective careers which ran more or less
in parallel; the Yorkshireman made his first-class debut a year earlier
than David and played on for a couple of seasons longer: 'Geoffrey
had lovely hands and great balance, and he kept going – that's the
main thing. I loved watching him bat. We were similar players in that
we both had that hunger.' When Boycott was diagnosed with cancer
in 2002, David wrote to him: 'A bit of a tough wicket, Geoffrey, but
if anyone can play it, you can.' And he did.

But David struggled for batting form in a damp summer and only
just scraped his 1,000 runs, overshadowed by Roy Virgin who enjoyed a superb first full season with the county. He bowled a few more
overs – Bedi missed the early part of the Championship campaign as
India toured England – and Northamptonshire retained third place
in the final table, finishing strongly and not enjoying the best of luck
with the weather during the run in. One theory doing the rounds im-
plied that David's relatively modest return was down to the fact that,
in October 1973, he'd been told by the committee that 1975 would
be his benefit year after Watts in 1974, and money-making thoughts
were already uppermost in his mind. If so, he would make up for it
as the beneficiary twelve months later.

Around this time the facilities at Wantage Road, with the decaying
Ladies Stand (finally demolished in 1978 to make way for the new
pavilion) and players still having to troop across the ground to the
County Tavern for lunch, were, as Bedi claimed, lousy. Not forgetting the football pitch-cum-outfield which could make a laughing
stock of normally safe men in the deep – when the ball went bob-
bling down there in the general direction of Dye, David would be
announcing the odds: 'It's five-to-one against the Doc.' But it was
the people that made the club, not the paintwork. Turner the cricket
visionary, 'Sec' rather than 'Ken' even to David, doing his bit for
public relations over the tannoy: 'Please cover up your car windscreen
at the football end, it's putting off the batsman. Yes, you! I won't tell

you again.' Dennis Brookes, a quiet and courteous presence in the office as assistant secretary, the good cop to Turner's bad. Jack Jennings, getting the hypochondriacs back on the pitch whilst checking his racing selections. Jack Mercer in the scorebox, full of cricket lore and conjuring tricks, according to David 'a slightly mysterious figure whose London flat was like an old pavilion with jewels he'd been given playing for India in the 1930s kept in a tin.' He would leave the scorebox during the day's play and go for a walk, filling in the book with the help of his opposite number, and telling his tales with a watery-eyed laugh. And whistling – 'when anyone whistles now I still think of Jack.' And, up there in the signal box with Mercer, Fred Speakman, whose old coat was reputed to leave by itself at the end of the season. The warp and weft of Northamptonshire cricket, with David – by dint of performance and personality – earning the right to be part of it too.

6

DROUGHT, DISILLUSIONMENT AND DEPARTURE

The summer of 1976 produced the highest average temperatures since records began with water shortages so critical that, in August, the former Labour Sports Minister Denis Howell was appointed Minister for Drought. If the nation sweltered, its Test cricketers were to be subjected to heat of a different kind: that generated by the fearsome pace of the visiting West Indian bowling attack. The tour party may not have arrived in an aircraft piloted by Captain Tobias Willcock of Coconut Airways, but devotees of popular music will no doubt recall that Typically Tropical's 'Barbados' had topped the UK charts in August 1975. Sadly, the group was unable to repeat the achievement and, as the new season began, the cricketing world was interested to discover if another surprising success from the previous year would also turn out to be a 'one-hit wonder'.

David had enjoyed a stint in South Africa with Derrick Robins' touring team, scoring an unbeaten 110 at Cape Town against a powerful Western Province team including Eddie Barlow, Peter Kirsten, Garth le Roux and county teammates past and future, Hylton Ackerman and Allan Lamb. The *South African Cricket Annual*, however, declared itself puzzled that 'Steele made little attempt to shield the later batsmen' as the hosts won by taking two tail-end wickets in the final over, including Northamptonshire old boy Peter Lee first ball. Back home, David carried his form with the bat into the first two games of the County Championship season. An impressive 93 not out in a drawn match with Lancashire at Old Trafford in late April was followed by 139 at Lord's against Middlesex. But despite these apparent grounds for optimism, he wasn't happy with his game, citing a lack of sharpness, and his mood worsened when he barely troubled the scorers against Essex in his final match before the first Test at Trent Bridge.

After the West Indies had recorded an impressive first innings total of 494, with Viv Richards hitting a double century, England lost Mike Brearley before a run was scored and David marched out to the crease. Any self-doubts were quickly dispelled as he dug in for the long haul. During a brief lull in proceedings his batting partner, John Edrich, had walked down the wicket and confessed that he found batting against the West Indian quicks boring.

'I'm just so bloody fed up waiting for them – you stand there and it's all that length of time before the ball comes down.'

David had no such concern. 'It didn't bother me,' he recalls. 'I could wait all day.'

Edrich and he took the score to 98 before the Surrey opener was caught behind for 39 off Wayne Daniel. Brian Close then fell cheaply but David's partnership with Bob Woolmer flourished. There were a few anxious moments during that innings; a miscued hook early on that just cleared the fielder at square leg, a painful rap on the 'upper thigh' as he attempted to pull Andy Roberts and even a swarm of bees flying across the ground. With a century beckoning he chanced a risky second run and ended up having to dive full-length to make his ground, brushing off the mud and grass as he got to his feet. Then a Roberts no-ball, called by umpire Tom Spencer, was pulled behind square to the boundary. The holy grail of a Test hundred – frustratingly elusive in '75 – was his for keeps in '76. A little prototype fist-pump, more Dennis Taylor than Tiger Woods, a kiss of the cap badge and sheer delight etched on his face. 'My word, if any England batsman deserved a hundred in a Test match it has to be David Steele,'

En route to a Test century at Trent Bridge in 1976.

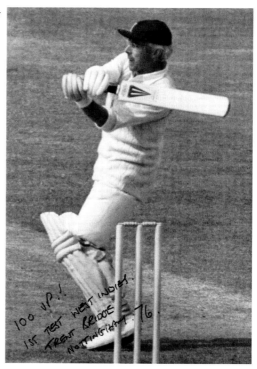

commentator Jim Laker told the TV audience. Moments later he was heading back to the pavilion at the close play, undefeated on 105 and visibly chuffed to bits. Next morning David added just a single from a sharp chance to the gully before another hook, this time at Wayne Daniel, flew to Roberts who held a simple catch at deep fine leg. He had made 106 on only his fourth appearance, the game ending in a draw.

For David there was sufficient time to help Northamptonshire to a four-wicket win over Glamorgan with a second innings knock of 60 not out, before it was off to Lord's for the second Test. David discerned a palpable change in the West Indians' attitude during the match, much of it, he believes, stemming from captain Tony Greig's ill-chosen comment that he was going to make the opposition 'grovel'. Whatever his intentions, Greig's words injected extra pace into the West Indian attack and, as David recalls, 'They were a couple of yards quicker against Tony'. He witnessed this at close hand during England's second innings when, adopting his characteristically calm, measured approach to building a score, the rather benign atmosphere changed with the arrival of Greig at the crease. The crowd became increasingly hostile, Roberts and Holding were in full cry and batting was suddenly a more dangerous occupation. David took the opportunity of a break between overs to register his feelings with his partner.

'I wish you hadn't bothered to come in,' he said, 'it was a good game until you arrived.'

David's innings of 64, which lasted almost four and a half hours, helped England set the West Indies a target of 323 to win. The game eventually petered out to a draw, but Greig did nothing to improve relations between the teams when insisting on playing out the final half hour even though there was little chance of either side winning. The stage was set for Old Trafford, but first there was the small matter of two County Championship games to fit in between Test match commitments, neither of which added significantly to David's ag-

Captain Tony Greig introduces David to the Queen during the Lord's Test. Also in the line up are Derek Underwood, John Snow, Chris Old, Barry Wood, Alan Knott, Graham Barlow and umpire Dickie Bird.

gregate score. Nought in an innings victory over Somerset and single figures in both knocks in a winning draw against Derbyshire was hardly the best preparation for events about to unfold in Manchester.

David played on two dangerous pitches against the West Indies: at Chesterfield in his Derbyshire days and at Old Trafford. Both were unforgettable experiences. The West Indies batted first and, with Test debutant Mike Selvey taking four wickets for 41, reached a modest total of 211, 134 coming off Gordon Greenidge's bat. In reply, Close fell cheaply and David went to the wicket with just nine runs on the board. In what proved a most unusual innings he quickly amassed 20 runs including three fours, off twenty-three deliveries, before being out lbw to his nemesis Roberts just ten minutes before the close of play. Although Trevor Bailey's newspaper report the following day referred to 'Steele's fine knock', David regretted his uncharacteristic flamboyance and his dismissal at 'just the wrong time for the team'. The following morning Michael Holding made short work of removing the remaining batsmen as England were bowled out for a paltry 71, David having top-scored.

The West Indies consolidated their lead in the second innings, Greenidge and Richards both hitting centuries, and declared late in the day setting England a mere 552 to win. David had felt unwell during the long stint in the field, his migraine worsened by the continual drumming of the beer cans around the ground, the soundtrack of that cricketing summer wherever the West Indians played. He approached Greig and asked if he could drop down the order as there was no way he could bat that evening; Woolmer was instructed to pad up in his stead. Recalling the scene David said, 'As he walked past, prepared to go out if a wicket fell, his face was whiter than my hair. "Bob," I said, "I'll do you a favour one day," and he replied, "I hope I live to see it."' That the openers, Edrich and Close, were able to put on 54 for the first wicket is testament to their bravery and skill as the West Indies pace triumvirate of Daniel, Roberts and Holding subjected them to a brutal and much-criticised examination on an increasingly cracked and unpredictable pitch. Edrich scored 24 in 142 minutes before being bowled by Daniel but Close, aged forty-five, soldiered on courageously, bounced and bombarded for almost three hours. 'He was brave as a lion, or else a bloody fool,' David recalls. 'He wanted to show them, just as he had Wes Hall and Charlie Griffith at Lord's back in 1963. It was ridiculous – as though they were bowling at a coconut shy. It seemed they didn't concentrate on getting Closey out – they were trying to knock his head off.'

Close had batted an hour for his first run, adding another 19 before his eventual dismissal by Roberts, and returned to the pavilion battered and bruised, where David witnessed the extent of his injuries.

'He always said that no cricket ball had been made that could hurt him, but I'd never seen anything like it. He was cut by the ball and bleeding through his shirt. But he just shrugged and said, "You should see the state of the ball!"'

Only Edrich, Close, Steele with 15, and Frank Hayes made double figures as the match was lost by the humiliating margin of 425 runs.

The fourth Test at Headingley followed just nine days later and the selectors made wholesale changes. Out went the heroic pair, Edrich and Close, plus Pat Pocock, Selvey and Mike Hendrick. In came Chris Balderstone, John Snow, Alan Ward, Bob Willis and David's fellow Northamptonshire all-rounder, Peter Willey. It would be the first time two players from the county had turned out for England together since Tyson and Andrew at Brisbane in 1954. On the journey north, David bumped into Sir Len and Lady Dorothy Hutton at a motorway service station. Hutton was a member of the selection committee that had, somewhat controversially, chosen the Northamptonshire man for the Lord's match in 1975 in which he had announced his arrival on the Test scene in such spectacular style. David relished such opportunities to spend time with the master.

'He was like a magnet. I had to be with him, listening, absorbing, he just loved batting and talking about batting. When I asked him about his thought process he said that he used to play in tens.' It was a similar approach to his fellow Yorkshireman, Dennis Brookes. He also referred to his top hand, the left, as 'life' and his bottom hand as 'death'. The analogy appealed to David: 'As a left hander when bowling and catching, but a right handed bat, my top hand is the stronger.'

Looking around the dressing room on the morning of the match David was annoyed to note that Woolmer was the only natural opener in the side.

'I couldn't believe we couldn't find an opener anywhere in England with all of county cricket to choose from. The previous evening Greigy had asked me to fill the bill and I said, "I'm doing a job for you at three, leave me be. They didn't ask Stanley Matthews to play centre-forward did they?" He put me in an awful position – I wasn't right. You get used to a routine and I'd been doing that since 1971. Whenever I'd had to go in early it didn't work and I didn't want it to work, but Greigy had picked me – I could so easily have missed out on Test cricket altogether, so I agreed.'

Patently, it didn't work again. David scored a total of just four runs in the two innings as England lost the match by 55 runs.

There was a brief return to county cricket and an end to his dry spell with the bat as 92 runs helped the team to an innings victory over Worcestershire, before the final Test at The Oval. David sat next

Sharing a smile with Viv Richards.

to Hutton at the pre-match evening meal and was privy to a couple of examples of the great man's dry sense of humour. When the beleaguered captain Tony Greig arrived Len greeted him with, 'Ah Tony, I see you still have the job.'

Over dinner the conversation turned to the weather, the discussion focusing on the summer's unrelenting heat. Another of the selectors, Alec Bedser, reminded his former captain of a particularly hot day in Adelaide when he was bowled for twenty-three eight-ball overs on the trot.

'I was so dehydrated I didn't have a piss for a week,' he complained. 'Why did you do that?'

Sir Len just smiled. 'Well, you were a good bowler, Alec.'

As David had sensed, Dennis Amiss was recalled to partner Woolmer and justified his selection in the most satisfying way by hitting a double century in England's first innings total of 435. That was in re-

Northamptonshire's history makers of 1976.
Back: Wayne Larkins, Geoff Cook, Peter Willey, Sarfraz Nawaz, Alan Hodgson, George Sharp, Bishan Bedi.
Front: Richard Williams, Roy Virgin, Mushtaq Mohammad, David Steele, John Dye.

ply to the West Indies' mammoth score of 687 for seven declared, the ball streaking time and again over the parched outfield. David contributed 44 before falling lbw to Holding, who finished with eight for 92. Declaring their second innings on 182 for no wicket, the West Indians set a target of 435 to win. England never came close, Holding adding a further six victims to his impressive bowling figures, and were dismissed for 201. David scored 42, batted for just over three hours and shared a brave but ultimately unavailing rearguard action with Alan Knott.

The series was lost 3-0, but although David had been less successful than against Australia the previous year, he was England's leading scorer with 308 runs at an average of 30.80. Surely that was 308 reasons why he could await the selectors' pick for the winter tour of India with a degree of confidence.

The day after the game finished at The Oval, David joined his county colleagues for the Gillette Cup semi-final against Hampshire at Southampton, but in a move still debated by supporters decades later, was not selected to play. Mushtaq's men had enjoyed a relatively smooth passage thus far, receiving a bye into the second round where they scrambled an eight-run win over Nottinghamshire, and then beating Minor Counties side Hertfordshire comfortably in the quarters.

Hampshire's 215 for seven seemed far too few as Roy Virgin and Peter Willey took the score to 83 for nought. 180 for three became 202 for four until, with two overs remaining and four wickets in hand, just six runs were required. The penultimate over produced one run and two wickets. Six balls to go and five still needed. The fifth ball of the final over saw Bishan Bedi somewhat fortuitously drive John Rice to the boundary and Northamptonshire were through to their first Gillette final.

Celebrations? Definitely. But would the side have panicked with the bat had David been there in the middle order? This was, perhaps, the first hint of dissatisfaction with Mushtaq's captaincy. Ken Turner claimed to have puffed his way through seventy-two Senior Service cigarettes that day and blamed the skipper – specifically, his decision to leave out England's national hero – for most of them.

There was no such omission for the final, played at Lord's on 4 September against the favourites Lancashire. They posted 195 for seven, largely due to David Hughes slogging Bedi's final over for 26 runs, but the old head's 24 grafted runs helped steer Northamptonshire to a famous four-wicket victory – the club's first major trophy, seventy-one years after gaining first-class status.

The Championship season ended with a convincing win over Yorkshire at Scarborough, David making 41 and 33, to round off satisfying campaigns for both club and player. The county had finished runners-up, sixteen points behind Middlesex, their best position since 1965, and won the Gillette Cup. David had consolidated his position as a reliable run-getter against the most formidable pace attack in world cricket. But, as events transpired, his security proved illusory.

After a golden summer, the storm clouds were gathering over Wantage Road and David's all-too-brief Test career was about to come to a shuddering stop. He had been chosen for the first of three one-day internationals against West Indies, all of which were lost, and the outing at Scarborough was his last match as an England player – and twenty-year-old Ian Botham's first. Graham Barlow of Middlesex and Nottinghamshire's Derek Randall were drafted into the team for all three matches and, when the squad to tour India during the winter was eventually announced, both were included. Steele was not. Nor was his county teammate, Peter Willey. Apparently the selectors believed them to be inadequate players of spin but, in David's case, there may have been another reason.

The club's official history offers this explanation: 'There was a vague feeling that Steele in some way might not be a good tourist. Well, he was nicknamed "Crime" because he did not pay. But it is also known that neither Steele nor Crump, who were originally known as the Milk Machine Kids, were big drinkers or high livers. It is not difficult to buy popularity by rushing to buy a round at the bar: Steele was actually one of the most affable and easy-going men in cricket, and a victim of the game's pernicious rumour-mill. He could also play the spinners, dammit.'

Whatever the reasons, David's disappointment at his omission from the touring party still rankles.

'I should have gone there, and then to Australia (for the Centenary Test). Not many have been done down like me!'

*

In May 1977, shockwaves ripped through the game's establishment when Kerry Packer, an Australian media tycoon, announced that dozens of the world's leading players were contracted to play in his World Series Cricket tournament in direct competition with the Australian 1977-78 season. On a smaller scale, Turner's machinations behind the scenes at Wantage Road had seismic repercussions of their own. His conviction that Northamptonshire's long-term success was dependent upon making wholesale changes to the playing staff was not universally popular and led to what club historians have described as the 'Great Schism', culminating in a fractious extraordinary general meeting just before Christmas. The dismantling of the

Celebrating victory in the Gillette Cup: Steele, Sarfraz, Bedi, Mushtaq, Willey, Hodgson, Larkins, Sharp, Dye and Cook.

team began at a committee meeting in late-July with the decision to release John Dye and Bishan Bedi, while the futures of Mushtaq and Roy Virgin were discussed but deferred. Further rumblings about the Pakistani star's captaincy were compounded when news belatedly reached Turner of his involvement in the Packer circus, and the secretary's patience was exhausted. He began negotiating Jim Watts' return as captain and planned to bring in South African Peter Kirsten as the club's overseas player.

Whatever his perceived shortcomings as a leader, Mushtaq's value as a player remained undiminished during 1977. He scored 115 in his first innings of the season against Nottinghamshire and hit three more centuries during the summer before signing off with 112 at Chelmsford in what proved to be his final game for the club. Well aware of the antagonism against him, he had relinquished the captaincy in August (David once again assuming the caretaker role), shortly after scoring 118 and 79 against Somerset. David and he had forged an enduring friendship over the twelve years they played together at Northampton; indeed David continues to hold his team-

Northamptonshire's famous five of the mid-1970s:
Steele, Willey, Bedi, Mushtaq and Sarfraz.

mate in great esteem, regarding him as 'the best I ever played with'. That there was mutual respect is evident from Mushtaq's own testimony:

> When I got to know 'Steeley' I soon realised he loved his cricket, worked hard at it, gave his life to the game and, quite simply, cricket was everything to him and I admired him for that dedication to the game and especially batting.
>
> As a cricketer, he was a great team man, a good fielder close to the wicket and an incredibly determined batsman. I never saw him back away from any fast bowler, he would always take them on, whether it was Andy Roberts, Peter Lever, Mike Hendrick, Mike Procter, Bob Willis – whoever they were or however great their reputations, Steeley never backed away from those guys and faced up to any challenge – as we saw against Australia, too.
>
> Robin Jackman pinned him on the ear with a bouncer one day. He had to leave the field but still came back on later and scored runs. That was typical David Steele. He was unlucky not to have played for England much earlier.
>
> He wasn't a glamorous batsman but he got the job done. He wasn't a six-hitter who wooed the spectators, he accumulated with nice drives and a solid technique. Every team needs those types of players and he was very good at what he did. We very much appreciated the role he played at Northamptonshire.
>
> He had a great sense of humour and usually it was connected to his attitude towards not spending money. He once ran me out against Leicestershire. He came to me later on and said, 'Mushy, I'm sorry. I'm going to make it up to you and take you out for dinner tonight.' I couldn't believe it. I thought, 'Wow, Steeley is taking me out for dinner!' So later we went out and I found myself in this long queue. I asked him, 'Steeley, what's this queue all about?' It turns out we were having fish and chips from the chippy! We all loved him for the way he was, he didn't change for anybody and he's a very likeable man.

In the event, David's second tenure as captain was short-lived. His first match in charge, a five-wicket defeat by Hampshire at the end of August and played under the one innings rule, was followed by a drawn game at Grace Road. A rare injury suffered during the match brought his campaign to a premature end, allowing Geoff Cook to take over for the last two fixtures of the season.

During the close season David divided his energies between fulfilling his familiar role as a sales executive with Staples Press, a printing company based in Kettering, and renovating a run-down house he'd bought in the nearby village of Geddington. He was oblivious to happenings at Wantage Road. Single-minded as ever, cricketing politics left him cold. The game was about batting, bowling and fielding. But discontent continued to fester amongst a large faction of club members culminating in the formation of an action group determined to challenge Turner's plans. Matters came to a head at the EGM when the committee's case, bolstered by a timely and persuasive intervention by captain–in-waiting Watts, eventually prevailed. It was argued that evolution, with the introduction of new, young blood, would prove cost-effective and secure the club's future. When the team took to the field for its opening game of 1978, of the players that had appeared in the corresponding match the previous year, only Cook, Willey, Larkins, Sharp and David remained. In had come Watts, Richard Williams, Tim Lamb, Alan Hodgson, Jim Griffiths and the new overseas player: not Peter Kirsten, but Allan Lamb.

David was not unfamiliar with the young South African. In 1970 he had taken a post coaching cricket at the prestigious Wynberg Boys' High School in Cape Town. On his first morning he arrived at the school's beautifully appointed grounds, set down his bag, and surveyed the scene. He was joined by Jimmy Matthews, the master-in-charge of cricket, who asked him what he was thinking.

'That lad over there,' he said, pointing out a boy batting in the nets. 'What's his name?'

'That's AL. The first eleven captain.'

'He's a very good player,' David replied. 'I shan't be coaching him too much. I don't want to spoil him.'

When reminded of his time coaching at Wynberg, Allan Lamb is somewhat scornful of David's influence. 'Coach?' he says, 'You didn't coach me.'

'I let you bowl, didn't I?'

'You did. You made me bowl all day, but only to give *you* batting practice.'

There's little doubt that Lamb matured into one of England's finest batsmen, described by David as 'simply a wonderful player'.

The 1978 season was regarded by some as the worst in Northamptonshire's history. The side finished bottom of the Championship table for the first time in thirty years, winning just two matches with six lost and twelve drawn. The picture was no prettier in the one-day stuff either. David's form, like that of his teammates, fluctuated throughout the campaign but he topped the bowling averages and enjoyed occasional success with the bat. He reserved his outstanding performances for the two games against Derbyshire. The first, at Northampton in late June, was a match-winning display in which he contributed 130 to a partnership of 279 with opener Geoff Cook in Northamptonshire's first innings total of 344 for four. He then took six for 36 and five for 39 as Derbyshire were defeated by an innings and 40 runs. In the return fixture at Derby a few weeks later he scored 71, then 82 in an unbroken stand of 136 with Lamb. It's unlikely that these impressive figures escaped the notice of the Derbyshire captain Eddie Barlow and the club's committee, and may well have shaped future events.

It wasn't a happy return for Watts. Struggling to re-adapt to the physical rigours of the county game, he suffered personal tragedy with the illness and subsequent death of his first wife. Throughout this bleak period, David was determined to support his old friend as much as possible. Watts remembers one night, on the away trip to Cardiff, when sleep proved elusive as he dwelt on his personal troubles. David offered a sympathetic ear: 'If we're still awake at four o'clock, we'll go out for a walk in Sophia Gardens.' In the event it wasn't necessary, but forty years on Watts is still grateful to his old friend and teammate for helping to ease the pain a little.

For Watts, and for Northamptonshire, there were brighter times ahead. But David would have to wait three years before he could enjoy a swansong with a revitalised squad at Wantage Road.

7

A TEMPORARY PEAKITE

One of David's favourite aphorisms, borrowed from his father, main-tains that, 'You meet a lot of people in your life. Most you forget. Some you never do.' Of the memorable characters that David en-countered during his days at Northampton, two in particular retain a special place in his affection.

Dennis Brookes joined Northamptonshire in 1934 and amassed almost 30,000 runs, a county record, in a first-class career that ex-tended until 1959. He was second eleven captain when the young Steele arrived four years later and the two forged an enduring friend-ship. David recalls visiting Dennis's home in the months before his death in 2006: 'The terraced house in Wantage Road resembled a cricket changing room, was stacked full of memorabilia and was none too warm. When I started rubbing my hands together Dennis, a true Yorkshireman and frugal to the end, would say, "If you're cold, keep moving around."'

During the final years of his life, the elder statesman would retrace the steps he'd covered hundreds of times before to the nearby County Ground, aided by his zimmer frame, and circle the boundary casting watchful eyes over proceedings in the middle. The place had been his life and he had acted as a respected 'critical friend' to generations of cricketers, keen to tap into his deep-rooted knowledge and under-standing of the game. David was one such beneficiary:

> It was August 1967. I was going through a bad patch with the bat at the time and had taken myself off to nearby Abington Park for a bit of soul-searching before travelling to Leyton for the game against Essex. Sitting on the park bench, deep in thought, I saw Dennis's unmistakable figure approaching, dog on a lead. He asked me what I was doing and I explained about the run drought.
>
> 'There's no road without a bend,' he said cryptically. 'It'll change,' and walked on.
>
> The words stayed with me. In our first innings I was dropped on five and went on to make 92. 'Thank you Dennis,' I thought. 'I've rounded the bend.'

The other character David remembers fondly got off to a bad start with him. One morning, not long after his arrival at Northampton, David answered the telephone in the pavilion. Confident that he'd correctly identified the voice at the other end he asked, rather chirpily, 'Is that you, Ken?'

The familiarity was not well received.

'What do you mean, *Ken*!' he retorted, scarcely concealing his annoyance. Thereafter, Mr Kenneth Turner was always 'The Sec'.

Turner had arrived at Northamptonshire in October 1949 for a two-month trial as assistant secretary to retired army officer Lieutenant-Colonel Alleyne St George Coldwell, taking over the senior role nine years later. In the club's official history he is credited, along with Freddie Brown, with transforming Northamptonshire into a modern, successful cricket club. Frank Tyson's 'Personal View', an insightful foreword to the same publication, describes Ken as 'Northamptonshire's chief head-hunter' whose 'seek and enlist' campaign brought 'a galaxy of international stars' and 'overlooked players and promising Minor Counties and second eleven talents' to the county from all points of the compass. Among them was DS Steele.

Over the years, David's relationship with The Sec developed into something akin to a professional friendship. He acknowledges that

Ken's reputation for plain speaking and curtness could frequently alienate and upset the very people he needed on side. David attributes this brusqueness to his reserved, buttoned-down personality. 'He was unconfident with people,' he explains, 'but I know he liked me and I would have loved to have known him better. Throughout my career he gave me crucial support just when it was needed.'

During the summer of 1978, David became increasingly unsettled at Northampton. His omission from the England touring party to India two years earlier still rankled and, in the aftermath of disappointment and after fifteen years at Wantage Road, he felt the need for a break. One morning he was summoned to the office where Ken Turner was holding an interview with a prospective young player and the youth's father. If he was expected to bear testimony to the virtues of Northamptonshire cricket, he didn't let the secretary down: 'Despite my unhappy state of mind I described the county in glowing terms. I was grateful for the many enjoyable and productive years spent at the club and certainly bore no malice.' Incidentally, the youngster's name was Kim Barnett, a future Derbyshire stalwart and England cricketer.

Later that year David received a phone call from Eddie Barlow, the South African all-rounder and then captain of Derbyshire. He announced that he was not returning for the 1979 season and suggested that David might accept the position in his stead. Captaincy had never appealed. The burden of responsibility would weigh heavily upon a player who just wanted to bat, bowl and field, concerned only with his own game and his initial inclination was to turn the opportunity down, as he'd done at Northamptonshire. As he recalls, 'I didn't want it, but the financial package was too good to resist. Anyway, I was ready for a change.'

He discussed the situation with Ken Turner who was totally sympathetic. 'Good luck to you, Steeley,' he said, before adding an important rider which neither party would forget. 'Remember, you can always come back.'

The public image of David Steele the cricketer, his dogged determination and fierce competitive spirit, was shaped during that

A model cricketer – now a familiar name, David is recruited to don knitwear for an advert.

famous Lord's debut in 1975. These qualities are laudable, coveted even, when watching him build an innings, trundle in over after over on a flat pitch or fielding within a whisker of the bat. But how do his physical bravery, mental toughness, single-mindedness or metro-nomic concentration transfer to the world beyond the square where different sensibilities are required? He was about to find out.

In April 1979, David met his new teammates in the pavilion at Derby for pre-season training and soon realised that his task in main-taining the progress made by his predecessor would be difficult. 'Ed-die had done a great job and was widely respected. He was a god-like figure to the less confident players, a 110 per cent man, always on the go, a fitness fanatic whose idea of the ideal training session was to go out running in the pouring rain.' But Barlow had gone and his ghost had to be thoroughly exorcised. David realised that his ideas would take time to be approved but placed his faith in the tried-and-tested methods that had served him so well over his long career.

'Never mind running up hills and dales, it was back to the nets. Everyone should be able to bat, including those right down the order. I told the bowlers in no uncertain terms, "You carry your bats around but never use them. They're just pieces of furniture." I even used my old friend and Staffordshire teammate, Bob Taylor, as an example. He was a wonderful wicketkeeper but for many years Alan Knott was preferred for the England team because he scored more runs.'

During what proved a short-lived stint as captain he had adopted the exemplary approach – 'show them you can play' – borrowed from Uncle Stanley Crump. He got off to a good start, hitting 74 not out in the season's opener against Leicestershire, having confidently elevated himself above Peter Kirsten in the batting order, but by early July he had relinquished the captaincy having acknowledged his unsuitability for the role. *Wisden* recorded: 'As a player he [David] earned the utmost admiration for his all-round ability and dedicated approach, but he found leadership foreign to him.' It cited in evidence the Championship match against Middlesex in June when, after Derbyshire declined to take up Clive Radley's challenge of scoring 215 in three hours – and the captain batted forty-nine overs for 66 not out – he was jeered from the field by the home crowd. The club found it necessary to put out a statement stating this was 'not in accord with their policy of playing purposeful cricket'. David's apologetic explanation some time later focused on his annoyance at the Middlesex pace attack bouncing his own tail-enders in Derbyshire's first innings. Some Northamptonshire supporters, watching from afar and still faintly incredulous at his decision to lead a 'strange' county when he had clearly never wished to skipper his own, shook their heads and smiled to themselves.

'Captains sacrifice their own ability for the good of the team and often their own game suffers. I didn't enjoy it,' David recalls. His unhappiness was recognised by Derbyshire committee member, the former player and Test umpire Charlie Elliott, who recommended he resign the position – to be succeeded by Geoff Miller – and concentrate on his own performance. It proved valuable advice. Once freed from the responsibility of leadership David's love of the game returned and he retains treasured memories of his days at Derby. This obsession with his own performance often obscured the bigger picture and he lacked the man-management skills essential in a leadership role.

Coincidentally, there are parallels with his work in the print trade, as son Arran has observed: 'A naturally gifted salesman, he followed his own instincts, often without consultation, in his determination to get the deal. He'd take himself off to meet clients, often ignoring the requirement to attend important meetings at head office – unmanageable, but operating with great effect within his own one-dimensional bubble. All very positive provided he was surrounded by good people.' The conclusion must be that while his individual contribution in both arenas was immense he was patently a reluctant team player.

Two of the most important members of staff at any cricket club are its coach and groundsman, and Derbyshire had fine examples of both. A former opening batsman, Denis Smith had enjoyed a successful playing career with his native county. He made two Test appearances for England in 1935 and held Derbyshire's records for career aggregate runs and number of centuries scored until both were overtaken by Kim Barnett during the 1990s. In his role as club coach he had watched the young Steele at Newcastle and been instrumental in organising his visit to the Derby 'Indoor School' before David elected to join Northamptonshire. On his arrival at the county in 1979, David was delighted to renew his acquaintance with a man 'who had cricket running through his veins'.

Denis was inseparable from head groundsman, Walter Goodyear. Walter had joined the groundstaff at Queen's Park Chesterfield in 1931, aged fourteen, moved to Derby seven years later, and with the exception of the war years, continued to serve the county until his retirement in March 1982. His wickets, as David recalls, had a tendency to favour seam bowling.

'On one occasion I walked out onto the square with Walter and looked in vain for the strip. "Where's the wicket for today?" I asked. "Just there," he replied. "That's green," I said, raising my eyebrows at the rather luxuriant growth. His answer contained incontrovertible truths. "Grass is always green. Same for both sides. Put the sticks in and let's play."'

Sadly, the double act came to an end in September 1979 when Denis died at the age of seventy-two. His wife Mary asked for the ashes to be scattered on the square where he had enjoyed such great success and, fittingly, Walter was charged with carrying out her wishes. The appointed day was cold and blustery and, watched by a respectful group of players and staff, Walter set off, urn in hand and dressed in his familiar mac and empire-line trousers, to 'put the old boy to rest'. When he reached the wicket he lifted the lid and was immediately caught in a powerful gust. On his arrival back at the pavilion the onlookers enquired how it had gone.

'Wind got up,' he replied forlornly. 'I've got more of Denis in my turn-ups than on the wicket.'

For some time after, the groundsman's cheery, 'Morning Steeley,' received the following reply: 'Morning Denis.'

There was no shortage of characters on the playing staff either. Several were prominent during a memorable match at Chesterfield in May 1980. The opposition was the touring West Indian side which was, apparently, on a huge bonus to win every game. Derbyshire batted first on a damp wicket with openers Barry Wood and John Wright first to face the formidable pace of Andy Roberts and Malcolm Marshall. Wood had arrived at the beginning of the season from Lancashire and David recalls both the all-rounder's cricketing talents and his bouncy, somewhat bumptious personality.

'Before he went out to bat he put on his helmet but shouted an instruction to the twelfth man. "Twelfthers, my floppy cap's there. I'll need it in half an hour." I couldn't resist firing a response. "Woody, if bullshit was rubber, you'd bounce to the moon."'

Andy Roberts' third ball of the innings hit the track, rose vertically, struck Wood on the side of his helmet and he toppled to the ground. After some time he got up, shaking, and was helped from the field. Back in the pavilion he was surrounded by concerned teammates who removed his pads and watched anxiously as he gradually came round. Meanwhile David had retrieved his floppy hat.

'It's not half an hour but you need it now,' he said as he wrapped the soft fabric around Wood's bleeding ear.

Was the blood on his hands an omen, he wondered, with the news that Wood's replacement, Peter Kirsten, was out. Minutes later David was standing at the non-striker's end, helmet-less and bespectacled, as another fiery delivery from Roberts struck John Wright on the head.

'I walked down the wicket and enquired how he was. His helmet had provided vital protection but he said that the noise inside was like a loud bell ringing. Remarkably, he recovered to make 96 in what was the best innings I've ever seen.'

A few balls later David was hit and, to the annoyance of umpire David Constant, he kicked the ball away in fury.

'Hold on, now then, that's not cricket,' the official exclaimed.

'Nor's that,' the batsman retorted angrily, 'this wicket's rubbish!'

Derbyshire 1981.
Back: Peter Kirsten, Kim Barnett, Colin Tunnicliffe, Steve Oldham, Paul Newman, John Wright, Alan Hill. Front: Geoff Miller, Bob Taylor, Barry Wood, David Steele, Mike Hendrick.

Returning to the pavilion at lunchtime, David removed his glasses but 'could only see stars, the tension was so great'. Having defied the quicks it was something of an anti-climax to be dismissed shortly after the break, caught by wicketkeeper Murray off medium-pacer Collis King for 31.

Given the hostile attack, Derbyshire achieved a laudable total of 229 and then restricted the visitors to a mere 290, Mike Hendrick ending an impressive spell of bowling with a hat-trick when David caught Joel Garner to bring the innings to a close. Sadly, Derbyshire collapsed in the second innings and were beaten by nine wickets.

David's relationship with Barry Wood developed and, as an admirer of the Yorkshireman's combative attributes and highly competitive leadership qualities, led to friendship, although this was strained somewhat by an incident that, according to David, happened in the autumn of 1981.

Barry had a riding stable in Cheshire and when a horse belonging to his wife had to be put down, David approached his former teammate about a replacement. Barry was happy to offer what he described as 'the ideal horse for her, a real gentleman named Zacharius.' A deposit of £50 was agreed, pending purchase subject to viewing, and Barry agreed to bring the animal down to David's home village of Geddington. He duly arrived and reversed the horse box into David's drive leading down to the stables, parked up, brought down the shutters and backed Zac out. As the hind legs appeared, David and his wife noticed that one was enveloped in a blood-stained bandage which extended up to the knee. Woody then turned the horse around to face the stable door. Instead of going through the opening, Zac proceeded to walk into the wall, prompting David to enquire if the animal needed to borrow his glasses. When Barry began to mention a price David quickly interrupted.

'Now's not the time to talk money, Woody. My vet, Angus Gordon, will be coming to give him the once-over in the morning.'

Barry left, and the following day the vet arrived to conduct his examination. His findings confirmed David's worst suspicions.

'He's about sixteen years old, half his teeth are missing and he's blind in one eye. Would you like me to shoot him now or are you taking him back to Cheshire?'

Zac went back. Knowing there was no chance of retrieving the £50 deposit, David was happy to take payment in kind from its disappointed owner – a dozen bales of hay and a Victorian hay-chaffer.

The 1981 season had ended with a memorable last-ball victory over Northamptonshire in the NatWest Trophy Final but the path to Lord's was not an easy one. Defending a small total in the quarter-final against Nottinghamshire, a combination of David's highly disciplined bowling and captain Barry Wood's bravery in fielding at silly point put concerted pressure on the dangerous Clive Rice, who was out played on. David also took the key wicket of Richard Hadlee, caught at deep square leg, and then held a catch off Wood's bowling to remove Basharat Hassan. To David's enduring disappointment his contribution was overlooked by adjudicator Brian Close when choosing his man of the match.

Collecting a second one-day winner's medal with a second county – Peter May does the honours after the 1981 NatWest Trophy final.

By the end of the season the demands of travelling to and from Derby were beginning to take their toll. A normal working day meant leaving home at around eight o'clock in the morning and arriving back thirteen hours later, fatigued and ready for bed, the only respite coming when the side was playing at Chesterfield and he stayed with Wright and Kirsten in their flat above a butcher's shop in the town. Having carefully weighed up his options, David found the perfect moment to make his next move.

In the immediate aftermath of the NatWest final he accosted Ken Turner and offered his commiserations.

'Hard luck Sec,' he said, before harking back to Turner's fond fare-well when he left Wantage Road in 1978. 'Any chance of me coming back next year?'

The secretary was true to his word. 'We've lost the match but got you back,' he replied.

8

BACK TO WANTAGE ROAD

On an April morning in 1982, David climbed the steps to the pavilion at Wantage Road and was greeted by his new teammates including his erstwhile verbal sparring partner, Peter Willey, just back from the first rebel England tour to South Africa.

'What do they think they're doing signing a old bugger like you?' Willey asked, in characteristically combative fashion.

'There's no substitute for experience, Peter,' David replied, 'and it doesn't come cheap. I must be getting twice as much as you.'

The bait was thrown and, to the delight of the onlookers, was quickly swallowed. The aggrieved Willey rushed off in the direction of the office and secretary Turner. Minutes later he returned looking sheepish.

'How did it go, Wills?' David asked, mischievously.

The reply was terse and to the point. 'He told me to f*** off,' he said.

David retains immense respect for the bluff and physically fearless all-rounder who he acknowledges was a wonderful cricketer. However, Willey's dour demeanour could make him the butt of his teammates' banter. Always subject to a painful knee, Willey favoured the use of adhesive bandages which he applied above and below the offending joint and ten to a dozen such rolls were ordered prior to the

Geoff Cook, the Northamptonshire captain who made full use of David as an all-rounder.

start of every season. Travelling down the M5 in a coach bound for a match at Worcester, David noticed smoke billowing from the distant Malvern Hills.

'Hey, Wills,' he said, pointing to the sky. 'Is that Sioux or Navaho or,' looking knowingly across the aisle at a complicit Ned Larkins, 'is it poor knee?'

Geoff Cook had assumed the captaincy in 1981 following Jim Watts' retirement, and had been around the club long enough to know that David had been denied the overs he craved by a succession of slow left-armers including Malcolm Scott, Dennis Breakwell and Bishan Bedi. So now was his chance. 'Geoff called me his "spinner-in-chief" and it was a role I relished. I was confident I could do the job, but my season started slowly in '82 and it was fourteen games before I got a return. Bristol had always been a lucky ground and so it proved once more.'

In the first innings of the game against Gloucestershire he took four wickets for 77 as the hosts were dismissed for 244.

That evening the players returned to their Bristol hotel where David was rooming with wicketkeeper George Sharp, a man he liked, 'despite his many annoying habits.' These, he maintains, included 'never making the tea, breaking wind at leisure and insisting on keeping the curtains closed during daylight hours'.

Relations between the two were severely strained by an incident early the following morning. Waking before his colleague, David adjourned to the bathroom, showered and shaved, and took the opportunity to explore George's washbag. He discovered a bottle of aftershave and treated himself to a splash or two. When he returned to the bedroom the powerful aroma soon woke the wicketkeeper who recognised the scent and reacted with fury.

'Have you used my aftershave?' he bawled. 'That cost Audrey £32 a bottle!'

David was unrepentant. 'Give over,' he replied. 'It's only aftershave. You can use mine. Anyway, why would she waste money on a face like yours?'

But the big man wouldn't let it rest. He kept complaining throughout breakfast, for much of the journey to the ground and during pre-match preparations in the dressing room. As the morning wore on the bad mood worsened, while outside at the wicket Northamptonshire's innings had collapsed from 257 for three to 287 for seven. David went to the crease, another wicket fell and he was joined by his new arch enemy, Sharp. To the relief of their teammates, professionalism triumphed. Their partnership of 76, with David unbeaten on 74, contributed to a total of 401 and, with the help of a further five wickets from the veteran spinner in Gloucester's second innings, the match was won by nine wickets.

David rates Cook's team as the best batting side he played in. Down at number seven, he was 'available if we collapsed, which didn't happen very often'. The position afforded him the opportunity to collect a number of not-outs, an asterisk – or red-inker – being 'one of my fantasies'. He scored 32 without dismissal in both innings against Lancashire at Old Trafford in July as his sequence of unbeaten innings stretched to six. The next match was against Gloucestershire at Northampton but, with the club record of eight in clear sight, he became uncharacteristically edgy, pacing the dressing room as he awaited the call to the wicket. He even lost a game of shove ha'penny to Captain Cook, a bad omen if ever there was one. His fragile disposition was recognised by former Northamptonshire fast bowler Lewis McGibbon – by now on the committee – who offered a glass of red wine to help steady the nerves. One became two and, when the next wicket fell, he strode out to the crease buoyed by this dose of unfamiliar Dutch courage. He was to face Barry Dudleston, a handy batsman but, according to David, 'something of a help-yourself bowler'. As he shaped to receive the first ball he played forward and felt his front leg collapse beneath him. The ball went through to keeper Jack Russell who completed a simple stumping.

David couldn't believe it. He looked down the wicket to umpire David Constant and implored him to 'give me another go', but the run was over and things were about to get worse. In the second innings he failed to pick Franklyn Stephenson's slower ball and was out lbw to complete his first pair in first-class cricket. Cook quickly summed up the dramatic change in fortune: 'You were the man they couldn't get out. Now you're the man they can!'

David ended the 1982 season with an outstanding return of sixty-seven Championship wickets at just over 24 runs apiece from 673.2 overs. At Eastbourne in August, on a pitch reported as 'unsatisfactory' by the umpires, David and Peter Willey shared eighteen wickets (the other two run out) as Northamptonshire triumphed in a day and a half. Value for money? Definitely. The county were boosted in their only innings at The Saffrons by a spectacular century from India's star all-rounder, Kapil Dev. His signing the previous year represented an obvious coup for the club – the only problem being that the committee wanted him to bowl, while he wanted to bat.

Cook has always denied that the decision to bring David back to Wantage Road had anything to do with sentiment: 'An easy few years to see out the dying embers of a fantastic charismatic career? A

Over and out: the final three years of his first-class career were the ones in which he bowled the most overs.

lap of honour at a club he had served proudly for so long? Neither was the case. The invitation was based on the need for the club to recruit some experience, and a new challenge was thrown down by the committee – "come back and bowl" they said. The placid wicket at the County Ground to a large extent dictated the type of cricket we started to play. Fast scoring, high scoring, declarations and run-chases became the norm. The seam department, while never lacking in effort, found the going tough at home. So spin it had to be.'

The theme continued in 1983 with David and the two off-spin-ners, Willey and Richard 'Chippy' Williams, delivering the best part of 1,500 Championship overs between them. If nothing else, it was a recipe for a healthy over rate – slowed only slightly by David's ir-ritating no-ball habit, 'a bit frustrating but sometimes very amusing' according to the captain. The bowler's explanation was always the same – eagerness to get at the batsman. His role in carrying the attack became that much more vital as Northamptonshire struggled to find an overseas quick bowler capable of cutting the mustard. Kapil's occasional appearances offered tantalising glimpses of the enormous talent and belief that made him a World Cup winner on one of Indian cricket's greatest days, at Lord's in June 1983; Zimbabwe-born James Carse, a regular with Eastern Province in South African domestic cricket and signed as cover for Kapil during the World Cup tournament, suffered a rib injury and played in fewer than half the Championship matches; the following summer Rupert 'Spook' Hanley, picked for South Africa against 'rebel' opposition, also struggled for fitness. David had coached Hanley as a schoolboy in Grahamstown and was disappointed to see the St Andrews College old boy suffer a string of injuries during his brief stint at the club. This quest for a pace bowling import was interrupted by David's retirement when, instead, they snapped up the West Indian off-spinner – and probably the best fielder in the world – Roger Harper for the 1985 season.

At the end of 1983, another old teammate flew the coop when Peter Willey rejected the one-year contract offered and joined Leicestershire. Ken Turner had been far from impressed with his public backing – along with Wayne Larkins and Jim Watts, the latter by then on the committee – for groundsman Les Bentley, dismissed by the club at the end of 1982. The case went to an industrial tribunal and (as it did following the sacking of Bedi five years earlier) the club won. Willey's departure cranked up the workload for David even more. He bowled 732 first-class overs in 1984, making it 2,165 in the three seasons since his return – not bad for a man past his fortieth birthday with a wobbly hip. The old boy could still score handy runs, too. Against Surrey at Wantage Road in July 1984 he and seventeen-year-old wicketkeeper David Ripley shared a century partnership for the sixth wicket against an attack including the fearsome West Indian paceman Sylvester Clarke. David was then forty-two and had been a capped Northamptonshire player before Ripley was born, a line too good to miss for the journalists in the press box. His young partner from Yorkshire would become another of the county's most popular adopted sons, staying on after a long and distinguished playing career to bring success – notably in Twenty20 cricket, which might not have been DS Steele's forte – as a shrewd and innovative coach. But even the teenager's toiletries weren't safe from David's attentions. Not Sharp's Old Spice this time, but acne lotion which Ripley claims the senior pro attempted to use as moisturiser. Another version of the tale says toothpaste, although Ripley admits that may have been a case of gilding the lily during some of his early forays into after-dinner speaking!

Raiding the contents of teammate's sponge bags wasn't the only old habit to die hard. Northamptonshire were battling to save the home match against Yorkshire after following on 194 behind and Chippy Williams showed just the kind of determined approach required. He battled his way to 35, at which point David 'did him like a kipper' over a single and Williams began the long walk back, run out. His understandably angry reaction entertained spectators and players alike, wafting his batting gloves in David's face as though challenging him to a duel. Unfazed, David duly got his asterisk – six, not out – in a crushing defeat.

It was, as Cook says, 'a fun team to play in – with Stanley Steele playing a major part.' Sharing a dressing room with him that season were the likes of Ripley, Rob Bailey (whose father John had turned out with David back in Staffordshire days), Cambridge blue Robin Boyd-Moss and a couple of Northampton lads, David Capel and Duncan Wild. It was a talented young side, good to watch and guaranteed to keep a forty-two-year-old fresh and enthused. But while the spirit was still willing the body was beginning to complain. What began at The Parks on 8 June 1963 ended in the shadow of Worcester Cathedral on 7 September 1984 – half a thousand first-class matches spanning six British Prime Ministers, from Harold Macmillan to Margaret Thatcher, and a bewildering array of social, technical, economic, political and cultural upheavals. When David went out to bat for Northamptonshire for the first time, The Beatles were number one in the charts with 'From Me to You'. When Worcestershire's Dipak Patel sent him back to the pavilion for the last time twenty one and a bit years later they were tuned in to George Michael's 'Careless Whisper'. It wasn't, but might have been, a reference to David's calling.

There was no fuss at the time, no avenue of players forming up to clap an emotional David in on his 500th and final appearance. His retirement wasn't announced to the cricketing public until a few days before Christmas 1984. 'Although he would find it hard to admit, DS Steele played through most of the 1985 season (a slip of the typing finger in Ken Turner's office, presumably) in physical discomfort arising from an arthritic condition in a hip,' noted the Northamptonshire yearbook. 'Notwithstanding this, he played in all twenty-five first-class matches. Such is the measure of the man. One of the last, if not the last, of the old-fashioned professionals, his service to the game has been outstanding. Your committee thank him for his services and wish him well for the future.' A common enough form of words used when a player won't be back on parade next season, but suffused with greater meaning in this instance. Writing in the *Guard-*

David with Northamptonshire in his final first-class season, 1984.
Back: Richard Williams, Neil Mallender, Rob Bailey, Jim Griffiths,
Rupert Hanley, Martin Bamber. Front: David Steele, Wayne Larkins,
Geoff Cook, George Sharp, Allan Lamb.

ian, the peerless Frank Keating delivered 'a heartfelt valediction to the pulpit' to mark David's exit from the county game:

> He played in eight consecutive home Tests against Australia and the West Indies – then both in their swaggeringly ferocious pomp – and never once flinched. It was a truly heroic and very human chapter in which David Steele tapped the sporting adrenalin in the whole nation. Yet, having weathered the fearful gales, he was then peremptorily put out to grass with a Test batting average of 42 – exactly the same as that of Ian Chappell and Cyril Washbrook, only a couple of pegs below Cowdrey and Graveney, and miles ahead of the likes of Woolley, Trumper or Bill Edrich.
>
> Steele must have felt disappointed when he was dropped for the 1977 tour of India. Characteristically he would have moaned only to the nearest short leg, but his legion of supporters – which included by then a considerable lobby of housewives who couldn't tell lbw from PVC – gave voice.
>
> The romantics, though, preferred him to leave on a high – the Indian spinners might well have shattered the image – and he waddled back to the county grind, garlanded with affection and remaining forever the personification of that authoritative pronouncement by Cliff Gladwin, another North Midland pro, who made the all-time anthologies with 'Cometh the hour, Cometh the man.'

David might have taken exception to the bit about the Indian spinners, but we'll let that pass. Keating ended a wonderful, tear-jerking tribute: 'Now, after twenty-one years of admiration around the provincial paddocks of England – 500 games, 22,346 runs, 623 wickets and 546 catches – he will be plodding away, just as he came into our consciousness those nine years ago – with that rolling gait of a strangely-armoured infantryman; jaw jutting, eyes slightly bewildered behind glinting specs, pad straps dangling, front foot forward. Thanks for the memory, Mr Steele. The way you touched your cap, the way you played for tea… no, no, they can't take that away from me.'

PART THREE

LANDSCAPING

9

Beyond the crease

In the early 1960s professional cricketers were contracted from April to September and had to fend for themselves during the remaining six months of the year. David spent his first two winters back in Stoke-on-Trent working in the printing trade. On Saturday nights, like many single young men of the time, he frequented the local dance hall where he indulged a new-found passion for ballroom dancing.

Some years earlier he had been encouraged by Stan Hulme, a teammate at Newcastle, to boost his range of social skills by taking lessons at a local dancing school run by a couple of trippers of the light fantastic named Syd Perkins and Edna Duffield. He caught the bus from Brown Edge and arrived at the hall where the sound of music confirmed that things were already in full swing. But, curiously, nerves began to fray and he couldn't find the courage to go in. Three times he approached the door only to turn away in fear. Finally he summoned sufficient confidence to push it open and step into the hall where he was quickly accosted by the dance master, Syd, resplendent in his shiny black patent leather shoes.

'Ah, it's your first time, isn't it? You'd better dance with my daughter,' said Syd, introducing an attractive girl who bore a distinct resemblance to the popular singer, Alma Cogan, complete with trademark beauty spot. David's early efforts provided few grounds for optimism but, having caught his partner's shins on numerous occasions, he was duly admonished by his teacher. 'David. I said you could dance with her. Not play football with her!'

Three lessons later he felt confident enough to take to the floor at Newcastle's Crystal Ballroom for the first time, dancing to Lennie Chell and his band. It was small steps at first. When one early partner had the temerity to interrupt his concentration by enquiring if the dance was a quickstep, he replied, 'Don't talk to me, I'm new to this.' Gradually, however basic techniques were mastered and the venue became a regular haunt. Strictly Steele.

The city was no stranger to dense fog, occasionally causing the cancellation of the buses on which David relied for a ride back to Brown Edge when the evening's dancing was over. On one such night he trudged the five miles home, reaching the outskirts of the village in the early hours of the morning. Exhausted, he collapsed into a ditch by the side of the road and slept under a hedge for several hours before being shaken awake by a familiar figure. It was the milkman, whose name really was Ernie, and he drove the fastest milk cart in Brown Edge. After hitching a lift David opened the front door and was greeted by his mother, who had sat up anxiously awaiting his arrival.

'Where have you been?' she asked.

'Two and a sterilised,' he replied, handing over three bottles of milk by way of explanation.

The lessons proved invaluable when he met Carol at Northampton's Salon Ballroom in 1964. Believing he cut an impressive figure on the dance floor, David was even bold enough to complain that she was 'a bit slow in the corners'. If that was hardly the most seductive of chat-up lines, a possible romance was further jeopardised when he discovered that she lived in Weldon, a village some twenty-five miles from Northampton.

'That's a long way,' he said, no doubt calculating the mileage and converting it into pounds, shillings and pence. Nevertheless, he offered to give Carol and her friend a lift home in the infamous Morris 1000 and then arranged to meet her again the following week. This time the pennies won and he didn't turn up. His decision might have brought things to an abrupt end but, fortunately, she was of a forgiving nature and the relationship eventually blossomed sufficiently for him to end his sojourn in Northampton's bedsit-land and move in with Carol and her parents at 37 Chapel Road.

In the autumn of 1966, Northamptonshire's opener and captain-elect, Roger Prideaux, had been unable to take up a position as coach at St Andrew's College in Grahamstown, near Port Elizabeth, and offered David the opportunity to take his place. It proved to be a fortuitous appointment and although the death of his mother, at the early age of fifty, prevented a return the following year, David was able to resume his duties at the college in subsequent years. Travelling back on the boat with Don Bates in the spring of 1970, the Sussex player mentioned that he wouldn't be renewing his contract at the Wynberg High School near Cape Town that winter. David was planning on getting married in September and thought the city location would be more attractive to his new bride. So, with the help of glowing references from Grahamstown, he put in an application for the

Carol and David – a successful partnership.

post. He was successful and, just three days after his wedding on 19 September 1970, Carol and he were on an ocean honeymoon bound for South Africa.

The couple continued to live with Carol's parents until they bought a bungalow in St Mary's Road, Kettering. There would be no more winters in the South African sunshine for some years. It was time to seek out a job in 'the real world' and, once more, David's father's insistence that he 'get a trade to his back' proved its worth. In April 1972 he presented himself at the Staples Printing Works in the town's Trafalgar Road and asked if there were any vacancies for compositors. The manager, Mr Pizzey, was summoned and after a few exploratory questions confirmed that there were.

'When can you start?' he asked.

'What about next Monday?' the eager applicant replied.

It was the beginning of a business relationship that lasted for fourteen highly productive years. After two years on the shop floor, David became a sales executive, travelling the country in search of contracts for his company. Among his early contacts was Hugh Winter, a print farmer with Centurion Press, an agency based in London's Burlington Street, which looked after companies' print literature. Hugh was a cricket lover from Kent and cultivated his association with the Northamptonshire all-rounder, especially when he stepped from the shadows of the county scene into the sunshine of the Test match arena.

However, not everyone was impressed by David's dramatic arrival on the big stage, as Alan Abbott, a work colleague at Staples Printers recalled. Writing in the *Northamptonshire County League Handbook*, of which he was editor, Alan described the rather underwhelmed response of David's foreman, one Jack Taylor.

Jack was from the old school of printing foremen, Victorian in his attitude of chasing people for not doing enough, making life as difficult as possible and very reluctant with any kind of praise.

When David worked there under his tyranny during the winter Jack would always be watching his every move.

'Come on Steeley,' he would grunt. 'Get on with your work, never mind talking about cricket. You've got all summer for that.'

Anyway, on the day of the Lord's Test, as I came back into work on the night shift, Jack was as dour as ever. Interested, but trying to make out he wasn't, he asked me the latest score. I told him and then even more dourly he grunted, 'How many did Steeley get?' By now I began to imagine he might genuinely be interested and told him quite excitedly that David had got fifty. 'Fifty,' he snarled. 'Fifty. Is that all?'

Of course when I told Steeley about this he loved it and always brings it up whenever I see him.

'Fifty,' he'll say. 'Fifty. Is that all? The man never did like me.'

But the nation did.

In December 1975 David received a phone call from the BBC informing him that the *Radio Times* public vote had placed him among the final three contenders for the Sports Personality of the Year Award, along with swimmer David Wilkie and athlete Alan Pascoe. Hearing this, David decided that perhaps he should accept the invitation to attend the event held, that year, at the BBC Television Centre in Shepherd's Bush. On his arrival he noticed three old cricketing friends from his Staffordshire days among the crowds thronging the foyer.

'What are you doing here?' he asked.

They explained that they'd entered a competition to pick *their* Sports Personality, giving reasons for the choice, and had won seats at the award ceremony. David didn't believe them. He knew then that he would be receiving the trophy. He sat alongside Ray Illingworth before being ushered to a seat on the end of the row and awaited the result of the vote. At last the announcements came.

In third place: David Wilkie.

In second place: Alan Pascoe.

And the winner of the Sports Personality of 1975: David Steele.

David spent the Sunday night in a hotel and the following morning went back to work as he'd decided to combine his trip to London with a visit to Centurion Press. On announcing his arrival at reception he was immediately confronted by an excited Hugh Winter who asked if he'd brought the trophy with him.

'It's in the car,' David replied.

'Well, bring it up and let's all see it,' Hugh ordered.

The impressive statuette was retrieved from the boot and carried aloft to Hugh's office where David made a mock presentation to the agent. 'You deserve this for services to the print industry.'

Hugh's response was something of a surprise. 'Can I borrow it for three weeks?' he asked.

Ever the salesman, David realised that loaning the trophy would have the potential to generate extra business for Staples Press. 'If you get it heavily insured, I can't see why not,' he replied.

David was eventually reunited with the trophy and it had pride of place on a table under the front window of his bungalow in St Mary's Road, alongside the Lord's Taverners award and the *Daily Express* Sportsman of the Year Cup. One afternoon his son Arran, who was just beginning to find his feet, toddled in the direction of the table, tottered over and reached out for support. He succeeded in grabbing

Receiving the BBC Sports Personality of the Year trophy from Lord Killanin.

the back end of the BBC's famous silver camera and breaking off a small chunk of metalwork. Uncertain what to do, David lifted the lid of the imposing *Daily Express* trophy and dropped the piece of silver inside. The following November he attended the newspaper's 1976 award ceremony where he duly handed over the cup to the new recipient, Grand Prix driver James Hunt. As it changed hands they could hear a rattling sound inside. Sheepishly, David lifted the lid and carefully retrieved the hitherto forgotten item. No doubt insurance covered the repair.

There is little doubt that David's new-found celebrity helped to open doors that might otherwise have remained firmly closed. One such door allowing entry into the National Gallery in Trafalgar Square was breached when his calling card reached its publicity department's print buyer. Gordon Booth, a Lancastrian and keen follower of cricket. He quickly made the connection between the name on the business card and the silver haired figure waiting at reception.

'Come in, lad,' he called, beckoning David to follow him to his office.

The three David Steels: businessman, cricketer and politician.

The pair soon struck up a friendly relationship which proved wholly beneficial. Staples Press printed the Gallery's brochure featuring 100 Great Masterpieces, sponsored by Coutts, and earned the company a goodly profit. David received his usual two per cent commission as a salesman. That September, his bonus was substantial enough for Stan Pizzey to remark, 'You've got more than me.'

'Ah,' said David. 'I planted the seed and then I looked after the job.'

Gordon Booth played host when Northamptonshire met Kent at Dartford in 1978, with the added enjoyment of watching his client hit 67 in the second innings before falling to a catch behind by Paul Downton off the bowling of Chris Tavare. Yes, Chris Tavare.

One of Staples' most profitable print runs originated from a rather unusual lunch date that David attended in 1976. He'd been invited by another David Steel, managing director of British Petroleum, to a meeting at Britannic House, the company's head office in Moor Lane, but was extremely curious as to why. On arrival he was conveyed in the lift to the top floor where a table had been prepared for three. He was then greeted by his namesake who gave no clue beyond saying, rather cryptically, that, 'the three Steels will meet.' After a short time the third diner appeared. It was David Steel MP, the newly elected leader of the Liberal Party, who also seemed somewhat bemused. By way of explanation, their host merely repeated, 'the three Steels will meet.'

David and his fellow guest enjoyed a splendid lunch with lively conversation but both remained wary, ever alert to the ulterior motive. It never came and when the politician left the cricketer took advantage by sharing a lift to Westminster. It seemed that their host had simply wanted to share a meal with his two famous namesakes at the height of their success.

However, a few weeks later, David was invited to tender for the printing of 50,000 copies of *The History of BP* and won the contract. It's not known what favour, if any, the future Baron Steel of Aikwood – first presiding officer of the Scottish Parliament – received.

10

BRUSHES WITH NOBILITY

In the course of his long playing career David became acquainted with cricket devotees from across the social spectrum. At the end of the lunch interval on the opening day of Northamptonshire's County Championship match against Hampshire in the summer of 1971, he and cousin Brian Crump were striding across the outfield from the County Hotel, when an impressive figure, impeccably dressed in city suit, came walking towards them.

'I think that's Jim Swanton,' David remarked. 'What's he doing here? He usually stays down south.'

The celebrated and hugely influential cricket correspondent of the *Daily Telegraph* approached the pair and, in that distinctively fruity voice so resonant with listeners to *Test Match Special*, enquired, 'Which one is Steele and which one is Crump?'

David was affronted at his ignorance and responded in combative style. 'Is this your first time in Northampton, Mr Swanton? This one here is Crump. He was five feet eight inches tall when he came to the county and he's now five feet six. He lost two inches bowling 12,000 overs in the past ten years. So I must be Steele.'

And the pair walked on.

The following year David arrived at The Parks in Oxford for Northamptonshire's match against the University side. Leaving the car park he arrived at the gates at the entrance to the ground at the same time as Swanton. This time recognition was mutual, formality dispensed with. Acknowledging the glorious setting on a beautiful May morning, EW began to declaim, 'David. England is a wonderful place from May to September. But after that, bye bye.'

'What do you mean, Jim?'

'I go to Barbados for the winter. And yourself?'

'Stoke-on-Trent. Do you know it, Jim? Coal, pots and Stanley Matthews.'

Had not the cricketing journalist, Alex Bannister, once written of Swanton, 'He's the biggest snob I've ever met. He had a chauffeur, but drove in the other car behind.' But as the conversation continued David began to overcome the initial antagonism fuelled by an instinctive aversion to his aristocratic bearing, public school accent and aloofness.

As David reflects, 'I began to warm to him. This was a man who, I later discovered, was a prisoner of the Japanese for three years, and whose survival in those dark days was partly sustained by his well-thumbed copy of a pre-war *Wisden*.'

David's performance with the bat that day would certainly have impressed the journalist. After Bob Cottam's eight-wicket haul had helped Northamptonshire dismiss the students for just 55, David hit 122 creating a sound foundation for the county's eventual victory by an innings and 105 runs.

At the end of the first day's play in the Lord's Test in 1975, the players were invited to drinks on the lawn by the secretary of the MCC. Among the dignitaries and media-men present was EW Swanton. Commenting on David's debut innings he remarked, 'They did say that you were a front-foot player, but you played some off the back foot today.'

'I've got two feet, Jim, and I can use them both,' David replied.

Press and media coverage of his arrival on the Test scene and subsequent successes against the Aussies during the series brought him to the notice of a wider audience and in the immediate wake of that glorious summer David became a national celebrity. His many

awards included, unsurprisingly, a place among *Wisden's* Cricketers
of the Year, the BBC Sports Personality trophy and recognition by the
British Council for the Rehabilitation of the Disabled as their Man
of the Year. The presentation took place the following September in
London and during the function he was introduced to the Society's
President, the Duke of Buccleuch. Unfazed by this brush with nobility, David embarked on a conversation in which he indulged his
mischievous sense of humour.

'Duke,' he began, 'I am your neighbour.'

Nonplussed by this unorthodox approach, the Duke raised his
eyebrows in surprise. His Northamptonshire country home, Boughton House, was situated in vast grounds equidistant between the villages of Weekley and Geddington.

David continued. 'My house, on the outskirts of Geddington, is
the nearest to you. There's just 2,000 acres between us. How is that
you missed *my* acre?'

*Brushes with cricket nobility. David with Colin Cowdrey, Cyril
Washbrook, Gordon Ross and EW Swanton.*

If the Duke was taken aback he soon regained his composure. 'My ancestors must have overlooked it,' he retorted, adding, 'But do you enjoy your acre?'

'I certainly do,' David replied.

'Then we're alright then.'

David acknowledged the swiftly considered riposte with an approving smile. 'I love your answer,' he said.

Some time later Carol Steele took a phone call, relaying the details to David.

'It's the Duke,' she whispered, shaking her head in bemusement.

'John Wayne?' David asked.

'No. It's the Duke of Buccleuch.'

His Grace addressed David like an old friend: 'There aren't many of us at the house at the moment. Just three or four family and a few staff,' he said, by way of explanation. 'I shall be passing by your home at eight o'clock on Monday morning. There's something I want to show you. I'll give you a blast on the horn.'

The Duke's car arrived at the appointed time and, to David's surprise, he produced an old cricket bat which he had apparently unearthed from a cupboard in an outhouse somewhere on his estate in Scotland. David inspected the wooden object with a critical eye then went back inside his house before returning clutching a bat of his own. It was one of several he and bat-maker Duncan Fearnley had taken to the Centenary Test Match in Australia and was embellished with the autographs of many of the great players attending the event – Bradman, Larwood, Compton and company – cricketing royalty. If he'd hoped to impress he was disappointed. There was no hint of recognition at the stellar signatures.

David returned his attention to the Duke's bat, carefully pointing out the differences with his own. He demonstrated that, whereas his was in two parts – a handle, spliced and glued into the blade, the Duke's was made out of a single piece of wood.

'Hit a ball with that and it would split in half,' he explained.

'So how much is it worth then?' asked one of Britain's richest men.

'Not very much,' the cricketer replied. 'It's made for the grate!'

David's association with Duncan Fearnley had begun in 1974 when, after failing to negotiate a more advantageous deal, he switched allegiance from Reg Simpson's Gunn and Moore brand to the Worcester-based firm. The move proved mutually beneficial as within a year the black symbol under the handle was prominent in countless photographs as a Steele straight bat stunted the Australian pace attack. In September 1981, David was invited to join Fearnley's Select, a team which included Ian Botham, David Gower, Graham Gooch and Geoff Miller, on a trip to the United States in support of Norman Gifford's testimonial. It also coincided with David's fortieth birthday. Billed as 'California Goes Cricket', the venture captured the spirit of Sir Charles Aubrey Smith, the former Sussex and England bowler and actor who, in 1932, had founded the Hollywood Cricket Club for fellow expatriates such as Laurence Olivier, David Niven and Leslie Howard. The squad were accommodated at the Ambassador Hotel in Los Angeles, home of the famous Cocoanut Grove night club and scene of the assassination of Senator Robert Kennedy in 1968.

The players and their wives enjoyed the hotel's ambience and its star-studded guest list. Carol was introduced to Christopher Lee, the British actor who had moved to Hollywood in 1977 in fear of becoming typecast. Tellingly, he agreed to sign an autograph as long as she didn't call him Dracula. Cheryl Ladd, a member of the fashionable Charlie's Angels, drifted by in the hotel lobby, but David had a closer brush with beauty when a shapely 'Friendly Greeting' turned up at his table to give him a celebratory birthday hug.

Matches were played at the Rose Bowl Stadium in nearby Pasadena, a venue more frequently associated with American football and capable of hosting crowds in excess of 80,000. There was a distinct lack of interest among the local community and the 3,000 or so Englishmen and women who watched the matches were lost in the banks of tiered seating. 'It would have been far better to have played them at baseball,' David recalls. 'We had some big hitters in our side.' One player stood out among the opposition, which was drawn from Hollywood's finest. When Lou Ferrigno, better known as the Incredible

Hulk, marched out to the crease, he was confronted by Ian Botham, who asked if he was wearing a box.

'What's a box?' asked the bemused actor.

'Something to put round your balls,' replied England's finest. 'But in your case you'd better get a dustbin lid!'

In September 1981, David was a member of the Derbyshire team bound for Lord's and the NatWest Final against Northamptonshire. As the players found their places on the coach, he spotted a distinguished-looking figure sitting on his own.

'Can I take the seat next to you?' he asked.

It was the beginning of an enjoyable and stimulating conversation with the county President, the Duke of Devonshire. Despite their very different backgrounds there were distinct similarities. A *Daily Telegraph* obituary following the Duke's death in 2004 describes him as 'humorous, self-deprecating and mildly eccentric'. These qualities could also be attributed to David. The miner's son and the aristocrat found further common ground in their love of cricket, the Duke anticipating the forthcoming match with undiluted excitement. More surprising was his readiness for self-revelation. 'When I look back,' he confessed, 'I was such a waste of a rich education.'

Referring to his days at Eton and Trinity College, the Duke once said, 'I was a horrible boy, lazy beyond belief, dirty, filthy, useless. Cambridge was a washout. Too near Newmarket.' It was the army, where his gallantry during the Second World War earned a Military Cross, which 'turned me from a useless boy into something approaching a man'.

David had put *his* education to good use in the quarter-final, bowling Derbyshire to an unlikely victory and, although less conspicuous in the final – five overs for 31 and skittled by Jim Griffiths for a duck – he gained considerable satisfaction from the defeat of his old county. When the medals were awarded at the end of the game his former teammate, the forthright Peter Willey, looked across and asked,

'What have you done today, Steeley?'

David, as ever, found the right response. 'Peter. What medal have you got? I picked up the gold.'

In the summer of 1984, David, now back with Northampton-shire, received a phone call from the Duke inviting him to play in a match at The Saffrons ground in Eastbourne, a town developed as a seaside resort by the Devonshire family during the nineteenth century. The occasion was to mark a hundred years of cricket in the town. The Duke had originally chosen Bob Taylor to captain his side against a Yorkshire eleven but, when the wicketkeeper announced his unavailability, he turned to his old travelling companion. The players and their families were accommodated at the five-star Chatsworth Hotel overnight and the game began on a warm Sunday afternoon. There was no shortage of talent on display and the presence of Brian Close in the Yorkshire team ensured a competitive encounter.

At the interval the Duke renewed his acquaintance with David, initially discussing the progress of the match but then straying to more esoteric matters.

'I'm off to Czechoslovakia next week. Have you been there?' His Grace asked.

'No, not recently,' David replied. 'I've been to Stoke-on-Trent. But it sounds an interesting trip. You'll enjoy it.'

The Duke pondered for a moment before adding, 'I'm leaving my wife to do the lawns.'

The game was won and before heading home the pair exchanged a few final words.

'David, when you next visit the Chatsworth Estate, give me a ring. You can come to tea.'

'Thank you. I'll do that.'

Unfortunately, his subsequent trips to the Derbyshire stately home proved fruitless. The Duke was never in.

In 1995, some ten years after David's retirement from the first-class game, an invitation arrived from Charles, the ninth Earl Spencer, to play for the Lord's Taverners against his eleven at Althorp House.

On the Sunday morning of the match, David drove through the imposing gates and down the tree-lined drive to the house and parked. No sooner had he arrived than he was greeted by an excited Charles Spencer who was clutching a copy of *Come in Number Three*, the autobiography compiled with the expert help of seasoned Northampton-based journalist John Morris in the aftermath of David's Ashes success twenty years before.

'I went to Maidwell School,' the Earl announced, 'and followed your career almost from its start to finish.'

'I didn't bore you to tears, then,' was the reply.

That the Earl had long hero-worshipped the 'no-nonsense son of Staffordshire' is evident from an article he contributed to *The Cricketer* magazine in July 2016 in which he extols David's virtues. Reflecting upon his introduction to the Test scene, Spencer recalls that, 'He got stuck in. During a very embarrassing run of results he was someone everyone could be proud of. I liked the whole thing about him: no frills, no fuss, totally committed ... It was the heroic side of Steele rather than any flamboyance that really touched the heartstrings ... He was a sweet, gentle cricketer and he came from an era before real professionalism and proper remuneration, where cricket was his life.'

As the article reveals, the pair met only once, during that match at Althorp, its charming cricket ground set among the estate's 13,000 acres. The Taverners batted first and David, who was then coaching at Oakham School and still playing the occasional game, was in good form. Going in at number five, he began to amass a tidy score, but was somewhat distracted by one of the umpires, a fellow member of his team. It was the unmistakable figure of the actor and cricket aficionado, Peter O'Toole, sporting a panama hat, a sweater slung over his shoulders and a cigarette holder and cheroot firmly gripped between his teeth.

O'Toole's lifelong love of the game had begun when, as a boy, he visited his local cinema and watched film of Len Hutton's marathon innings of 364 against Australia at The Oval in 1938. As his career in film and theatre developed, O'Toole was always keen to promote an understanding of the game amongst his fellow actors; even, it's reported, teaching Katharine Hepburn the basics on the set of *The Lion in Winter.*

Determined that his son, Lorcan, should be similarly smitten he enlisted the services of John Malfait, an outstanding coach with the Northamptonshire Cricket Association and later at the MCC, who took the youngster for training at Lord's. Then, to encourage Lorcan's appreciation of his own commitment to playing the game, he formed a cricket team, the Lazarusians, comprising actors and associates, while continuing to hone his own skills by attending nets under the guidance of Don Wilson, the former Yorkshire spinner and head coach at Lord's.

O'Toole often took part in charity matches at Althorp as a guest of Earl Spencer, insisting that, 'I open the batting, bowl two overs before lunch and field at slip.' On this occasion, however, he was taking his turn in carrying out official duties, striding from square-leg to the bowler's end and back but, to David's consternation, without uttering a single word.

Having reached fifty David decided that, given the occasion, he should give up his wicket and allow someone else the opportunity to bat. He proceeded to offer chances, lofting the occasional ball in the direction of the fielders. The tactic evoked a furious response from the celebrated thespian who broke his silence by declaiming in loud theatrical fashion, 'What the f***'s going on, Steeley? You're trying to get out. There's nothing else in the pavilion. Have some more!'

David took him at his word, going on to score a hundred before losing his wicket off Earl Spencer's bowling. The joy in dismissing his boyhood hero was palpable and provided Charles with a talking point for years to come.

David's association with the Lord's Taverners led to further meetings with members of the landed gentry. In 1996 he played alongside Francis, Lord Stafford, who captained the team against Rugby School. His side included the actor Robert Powell and star footballers Gary and Phil Neville (who had once played for the Lancashire Cricket Association against David's sons Arran and Mark), Coventry City goalkeeper Steve Ogrizovic and the peerless Jimmy Greaves. After his former Northamptonshire teammate Roy Virgin hit a century, and David, with a well-crafted 80, had built a commanding total, it was the school's turn to bat. Midway through the innings he tossed the ball to Greaves saying, 'Fancy a bowl, Jim?' The result was somewhat unexpected. The footballing maestro proceeded to turn the ball impressively evoking an enthusiastic response from his delighted captain, 'You're a natural, Jim. Bishan Greaves! I'll find you a turban at the end of the match.' There could be no finer praise than comparison with the great Northamptonshire and India spinner.

During the lunch interval, David engaged in conversation with the Taverners' President, Colin Cowdrey. He was keen to know how the genteel doyen of Kentish cricket had got on with dour Yorkshireman and former England great, Sir Leonard Hutton. Colin was forthcoming. He had been a freshman member of the England team that toured Australia in 1954-55 under Hutton's captaincy, and from whom he received an early dressing down. In one game he had been dismissed in his thirties and returned to the pavilion somewhat chastened.

'How did you get out?' the skipper asked.

'Bowled,' he replied.

Hutton shook his head gravely. 'Good players don't get bowled for 30. Nought or one, yes. But not thirty. You should be in by then.'

The message was clearly received. In the third match of the series at Melbourne, Cowdrey scored a maiden Test century as England recorded a crucial victory. It was possibly his finest ever innings in which he demonstrated the very qualities Hutton had demanded. In the words of Frank Tyson, 'Colin was icily superb. In four hours of batting his concentration never wavered.'

In the course of the day David built up a rapport with Lord Stafford, who invited him to address a Sportsmen's Dinner at the family home at Swynnerton Hall, near Stone, and then stay on for the night. Driving through the huge wrought iron gates leading to the estate, David noticed the Stafford knot interwoven into the metalwork. It was a poignant moment. The county symbol had been etched into his mind since childhood. It had emblazoned sweaters worn by the great SF Barnes and his Uncle Stanley's battered green cap. And now the boy from Brown Edge was the guest of the family which owned the crest.

The evening proved a success and the following morning he sat with Lord Stafford in the breakfast room inspecting a collection of fine Minton pottery which had been retrieved from the basement for cleaning. The irony of the occasion was not lost on David. Priceless items fired in the Pot Bank in the smoky heart of Stoke-on-Trent adorning a table in a stately home in rural Staffordshire. He, unlike them, had travelled a long way. Some weeks later David received a postcard from his aristocratic friend. It was a photograph of Swynnerton Hall, an imposing grade-one listed building, its three-storeyed edifice boasting fifty or more windows. An arrow pointed to one with the accompanying words: 'This is the room where you spent the night! Francis.'

But the meeting that surpassed them all occurred on a warm Sunday afternoon at Windsor where David appeared in a strong Taverners' team, including John Edrich, John Snow and regular, John Price. Out early, stumped down the leg side by Farouk Engineer, David had

Swynnerton Hall: the postcard sent to David by Lord Stafford.

Chatting with the Duke of Edinburgh, overseen by a royal minder.

taken some solace from a hearty lunch in the marquee. Noticing a familiar figure sitting in splendid isolation, but for an attendant, he walked over and introduced himself.

'Good afternoon, Duke, I'm David Steele. May I join you for a minute?'

The Duke of Edinburgh seemed pleased with the approach and quickly engaged in a lengthy conversation which revealed a love of cricket befitting his role as Patron of the Lord's Taverners, a position held since the organisation's inception in 1950. Apparently he had declined an invitation to become its inaugural President saying that it sounded too much like hard work. It was suggested that 'as every cricket team needs a Twelfth Man – to clean the kit, carry the drinks and generally stay in the pavilion and get sloshed – perhaps that would suit him better.' The idea appealed and the Duke has been Patron and Twelfth Man ever since.

No doubt reference was made to David's exchange with the Queen when presented to Her Majesty during the tea interval on the fourth day of the Lord's Test against West Indies in 1976.

'Are you enjoying it?' She asked.

'I am ma'am. There's 43 runs on the scoreboard and they're all mine.'

11

There's no business like show business

It's difficult to reconcile the player who became a by-word for dogged determination, whose intense concentration and focus whether batting, bowling or fielding was evident from his taut body language, with the fun-loving character that lurked within. There's little doubt that as serious as the game was during the 1960s and '70s, the opportunity for a laugh, usually at someone else's expense, was never far away. Sometimes, however, the joke would rebound and David found himself on the receiving end.

In the summer of 1972, Northamptonshire were on the verge of their historic success against the touring Australians. As we have seen, when Mushtaq fell with just 22 more runs needed David was joined at the crease by Brian Crump. Surely the boys from Stoke-on-Trent would see the side home? But that attempted single to Bruce Francis fielding in the deep proved fatal to Crump who was left hopelessly stranded. It made no difference to the outcome as David, partnered by Jim Watts, finished the job with no further alarms. Returning to the pavilion, David encountered a good-natured ribbing from his teammates led by long-serving physiotherapist, Jack Jennings.

'Fancy running your cousin out, Steeley,' he chuckled.

David's reply would not go unnoticed. 'Ah,' he said, 'that's show business, Jack.'

The next day, Northamptonshire and Middlesex began a County Championship match at Lord's. Settling into another promising partnership with Mushtaq, and with 36 runs to his name, David (who, unusually, had opened the innings with Geoff Cook) pushed the ball past point and set off for an easy single. To his surprise Mushy stayed put. David kept going, expecting his partner to cross, but the Pakistani didn't move. To his horror David found himself standing alongside Mushtaq at the non-striker's end while the Middlesex keeper, Jeff Hopkins, removed the bails at the other end.

David looked up to umpire Charlie Elliott for clemency. 'Give *him* out, Charlie!' he begged. 'He's the one that messed up.'

His plea fell on deaf ears. '*You're* out' said Elliott, raising his finger, and David faced the long walk back to the Lord's pavilion passing Hopkins, who was now tossing the ball from hand to hand and grinning inanely. The taunting further inflamed David who couldn't resist a comment.

'Jeff,' he said, through gritted teeth, 'I think you're enjoying this rather too much.' But possibly not as much as the reception committee thronging the famous balcony. On entering the dressing room he was greeted by his teammates, led by choir master Jack Jennings standing imperiously on a table, bawling out a resounding chorus of 'There's no business like show business'. The singing wasn't in the Ethel Merman class, but the point was made and the biter well and truly bit. Mushtaq went on to make a superb century – 110 undefeated runs in a modest-looking total of 250 all out, his only hundred at Lord's – and Middlesex collapsed twice in the equivalent of a single day's play to lose by an innings.

The list of run-out victims grew longer over the years, but one game surpassed all others. On Sunday 14 August 1977, Northamptonshire faced Essex in the John Player League at Wellingborough School. The visitors made 160 which, in the conditions, represented a decent score. Northamptonshire lost early wickets in reply but with opener Peter Willey in fine form it looked odds-on a home win. David went in to bat at number six and promptly ran out Willey, whose anger was palpable and unsurprising. A useful partnership with

George Sharp ended in similar fashion. With seven wickets down, 64 runs were still required for victory. Unmoved, David batted on with new partner Sarfraz Nawaz. It would prove a short-lived association. The Pakistani was another victim of David's eccentric running, out for two, and defeat then seemed inevitable. Back in the pavilion, captain Mushtaq was in despair crying, 'What's Steeley doing? He's destroying my team.' A flurry of runs from Alan Hodgson restored hopes but he eventually fell to a catch by Mike Denness with another 24 needed. David was joined at the crease by Bishan Bedi, a brilliant bowler but not the most reliable with the bat. He had little chance to use it as he soon became David's fourth run-out victim. Last man Jim Griffiths fell lbw to John Lever and the innings was over. All out 140, DS Steele not out 25.

As he left the field, the Essex players formed a cordon and clapped David off. He'd won them the match. But when he attempted to enter the Northamptonshire dressing room, the reception was altogether less enthusiastic. 'You can sod off!' was the politest greeting from behind the locked door.

'What about my kit?' he asked.

'Just go!' his teammates replied.

So he did, arriving home fully clad in flannels, shirt and sweater and wearing his pads and cap. 'Another not out today,' he announced to a bemused Carol.

Perhaps the most unfortunate casualty of David's 'misjudgements' was the Derbyshire and England all-rounder, Geoff Miller. During his long career, Geoff scored just two first-class centuries but reached fifty on seventy-two occasions. In 1981 the maiden century remained elusive and he approached David, then a Derbyshire player, for advice on how best to reach that cricketing milestone. The response was brief and to the point.

'Bat higher up the order,' he said. 'You'll struggle to get a ton going in at seven.'

Geoff took his words to heart and some time later, in a Championship match against Gloucestershire, he found himself batting alongside David, who recalled how well his teammate was playing.

'He looked in really good touch. I was feeling pretty confident myself having just passed 20,000 first-class runs, but he looked odds on to make a hundred that day.' There was probably no need to chase a quick single when Geoff played the ball behind the wicket, but David called and, realising it was tight, dived in at the wicketkeeper's end. Looking up he saw Jack Russell's moustachioed face staring down beneath his trademark floppy hat.

'Is that you, Jack?' he asked.

'You're in mate,' the keeper replied, 'but your partner doesn't look so happy.'

A disconsolate Miller, his dream of a hundred dashed in a split second, trudged from the field without a backward glance at the architect of his downfall. David played out the four overs remaining to close of play and returned to the pavilion where he was confronted by a most macabre sight. Swinging from a beam in the ceiling was a hangman's noose.

'He hasn't done it, has he?' David asked the gathering.

'He's left it for you,' they replied. 'He's in the bath and he's not a happy man.'

Knowing he had to confront the despairing Miller, David went through to the bathroom where he received a barrage of invective of which 'selfish bugger' was the recurring theme.

An uneasy silence prevailed after poor Miller had exhausted his lengthy list of expletives before David delivered his *coup de grace*.

'Geoff,' he said, adopting his most conciliatory tone, but edging ever closer to the door. 'It was like this. I knew I could get a hundred... but I didn't know about you.'

However, unbeknown to either player, there was to be a postscript.

In the last game of the season, Derbyshire faced Northamptonshire in the NatWest final at Lord's. In a tense finale, Derbyshire required seven runs to overtake their opponents' total off the last over. With just one ball remaining the deficit was reduced to two but, as batsmen Colin Tunnicliffe and Geoff Miller were aware, a single would be sufficient for victory under the fewer wickets rule. With Tunnicliffe about to face Jim Griffiths, Miller waited at the non-striker's end. The ball struck the batsman's pads and the pair scampered towards each other in a mad dash for the winning run. Meanwhile, Geoff Cook had fielded the ball and raced Miller to the stumps. There was a frantic dive for the crease, the bails were removed and eyes turned towards umpire Constant at square leg. Not out! The game was won by Derbyshire and Miller ran towards the pavilion, bat raised in triumph. Later that evening David sought out the ecstatic match-winner.

'Hey, Mills,' he said. 'I know that run out at Derby still rankles but may I say that it enabled you to gain the yard of pace that won us the trophy today.'

Earlier in David's spell at Derbyshire, Colin Tunnicliffe had inadvertently featured in another incident which revealed the all-rounder's sense of fun. During a match against Hampshire at Basingstoke in July 1979 he was no-balled several times by umpire David Halfyard, the former Kent and Nottinghamshire bowler. David was dumbfounded and challenged the official.

'You're over-stepping by three or four inches,' he explained.

'Forgive the pun, Dave,' Steele replied, 'but I don't want half a yard. Just give me an inch.'

It was to no avail. As the *Telegraph* correspondent, David Green, reported the next day, 'Steele, with an eagerness to get to the batsman, was no-balled twenty times.'

Determined that there should be no repetition in the next game, against Lancashire at Old Trafford, David adopted an unusual strategy. Foraging in the dressing room before the match he found a pair of boots belonging to Tunnicliffe who wasn't playing that day.

Selecting the left boot, which was several sizes larger than his own, he asked if he could borrow it, offering an improbable explanation.

'It's my anti-no-balling boot,' he told his incredulous teammates.

It was filled with padding, David slipped his foot inside, laced it up and, because it was difficult to negotiate the steps wearing the outsize boot, was carried down to the pitch by a phalanx of players.

For the first three overs his tactic seemed to be working. Aware of his enlarged foot, he kept well back from the crease until, midway through the fourth, he heard the dreaded call.

'No ball!' shouted umpire Bird.

'Impossible,' came the retort.

'Because?' enquired Dickie.

'Come and look at this,' the bowler replied, pointing out the giant boot. 'Does this sacrifice deserve no-balling?'

The famous Yorkshireman relented and David's stint ended with impressive figures of eight overs, one maiden, one wicket for 31. The bogey was nailed and the anti-no-balling boot ceremonially locked inside a glass trophy cabinet.

Cricket at its best is theatre, and one of theatre's most exciting components is drama. There was certainly no shortage of excitement when Glamorgan entertained Northamptonshire in a Championship match at Cardiff in June 1976. In a low-scoring game the visitors, requiring a mere 214 to win, were reduced to 114 for five when David was joined at the crease by wicketkeeper George Sharp. The pair faced a bowling attack comprising the West Indian quick, Gregory Armstrong, and Tanzanian medium pacer, John Solanky. Despite his side's precarious position, George played the latter with composure and began to amass a tidy score while David was coping less comfortably with the more hostile Armstrong. It was soon apparent that Sharp was happy for that arrangement to continue and, in a mid-wicket consultation with his batting partner, said as much. 'I'll play Solanky if you take Armstrong.'

The partnership yielded 79 precious runs before George, eventually exposed to the dangerously unpredictable West Indian, was out lbw for 56. Another 21 were still required to win, with runs increasingly difficult to come by. With David at his most obdurate, Northamptonshire inched their way towards the target until just four were needed for victory. Armstrong, who had consistently experienced difficulty finding a rhythmic run-up and bowling an inordinate number of no-balls, charged to the wicket and delivered, digging the ball in. It pitched, flew into in the air, sailed over the batsman's head, evaded the wicketkeeper's despairing leap, bounced once just short of the sightscreen and disappeared over the boundary bringing the match to a bizarre end.

In an attempt to explain his erratic delivery the bowler was philosophical. 'Man, I just lose my cool,' he said. His contract was terminated at the end of the season.

*

Desperate times require desperate measures, but nothing could ever compare with events during a Championship match against Warwickshire at Edgbaston in 1972. The hosts had been dismissed for 133 on the first day and David was in at the close of play. That evening, Bedi and Mushtaq decided to take a trip into the city centre to sample one of Birmingham's famed balti restaurants and invited David to join them. They even persuaded him to break with the habit of a lifetime and try a curry, promising that it would be of the mild variety and that they would pay. The lure of a free meal proved too strong for the reticent meat-and-two-veg gourmet and he eventually sat down to sample the tandoori chicken masala, forking the food reluctantly into his mouth despite its fiery ingredients setting his tongue alight. Later that night the discomfort had moved down to his stomach and by the next morning his bowels were churning and he felt desperately ill.

On arriving at the ground he spent his pre-match preparation sitting in the toilet, padded up, when the dreaded call came. 'Come on Steeley, it's time!'

He ran out determined to make his innings as brief as possible before returning to the comparative sanctity of the dressing room and its adjacent facility. Batting with complete abandon, he flashed the blade like never before and had soon knocked up a decent score. Standing at the non-striker's end, he realised that he was the object of fielder Mike Smith's concerned attention.

'Are you feeling unwell, David?' the Warwickshire man asked.

'Why do you ask?' the hapless batsman replied.

'Because you've messed yourself.'

Despite his uncharacteristic cavalier approach, he returned to the pavilion at lunchtime undefeated, still suffering but in more buoyant mood.

'Sixty not out with a burning arse!' he announced proudly, before disappearing into the toilet to apply copious amounts of talcum powder to the seat of his soiled trousers. He went on to make 107 not out and *Wisden* noted that his four-and-a-half-hour knock 'set the tempo for the Northamptonshire innings.' Rather a hectic one in some respects.

At Worcester, in August 1964, Northamptonshire encountered the peerless Tom Graveney batting on a perfect New Road pitch. Almost in desperation, captain Keith Andrew turned to David for a bowl. Graveney had reached 32 when David lured him into a rare false stroke. He edged behind and Andrew, widely regarded as one of England's most accomplished wicketkeepers, dropped a simple catch. It proved an expensive miss. Graveney went on to his century and, at the precise moment he achieved that score, the game stopped. The Worcestershire twelfth man entered the field of play bearing a silver salver, wine glasses and a bottle of champagne in celebration of what had proved to be the supreme batting stylist's hundredth hundred in first-class cricket.

In David's words it was an example of 'cricketing theatre' at its very best. When Graveney had extended his score to 132 he unaccountably repeated his earlier error, but this time Keith Andrew made no mistake. The bowler was quick to remind him of his profligacy. 'Well caught, Skip. Exactly a hundred runs too late.'

David's analysis that day of thirty-five overs, sixteen maidens, four wickets for 65 runs – in his second season of Championship cricket – was an early indication of his talents as an all-rounder.

Some years later, David and Tom Graveney were fellow spectators at the New Road ground. They began to reminisce and David asked if he remembered the day he scored his hundredth hundred after being dropped on 32, and who eventually took his wicket. Tom immediately excused himself and disappeared into the pavilion for a few minutes before returning, a copy of *Wisden* in hand.

'You're right, Steeley,' he said shaking his head in disbelief.

The conversation moved on to discuss the merits of the best bowlers they'd faced in their long careers. Both experienced the celebrated Australian and West Indian quicks but Tom also retained admiration for a certain Northamptonshire left-arm spinner.

'I was playing for Gloucestershire at the Wagon Works ground in Gloucester,' he said, 'and we were eight wickets down with George Tribe doing most of the damage. I'd got about seventy and noticed how he'd give me an easy single every time I got to the striker's end. I asked him why and he said, "Why would I want to bowl at you when I can get the others out so easily?"' The scorecard for that match, in 1958, shows Northamptonshire winning a tight contest by 16 runs; Graveney 55 not out in the first innings and run out for 112 in the second, as Tribe and fellow Australian spinner Jack Manning shared a dozen wickets in the game. It was Championship cricket at its best, and Tribe's comment a tribute from one maestro to another.

That's show business.

12

On tour

Following his remarkable success during the summer of 1975, David was disappointed that England were without a winter tour that year. The West Indies were eagerly awaited opponents during the summer of 1976 but he relished the opportunity to maintain his good form and was delighted to accept an invitation to join Derrick Robins' XI in South Africa, where he made that unbeaten century at Newlands but failed to shield the tail. The squad was captained by David 'Bumble' Lloyd with Ken Barrington as tour manager, and 'the Colonel' had already been appointed to fill a similar role with the MCC team for its trip to India the following winter. David was impressed by his man-management skills and looked forward to linking up with him again on the sub-continent. Sadly, it was not to be. After his heroics against the West Indies there could be little consolation for his omission from the touring party that travelled to India and then on to the Centenary Test against Australia at Melbourne in March 1977. David did attend that event, however, accompanying Duncan Fearnley on a business trip to promote sales of his bats.

Fellow passengers on the flight out included many former England players who had toured Australia over the years. The list of famous names was endless: Percy Fender, aged ninety-five, blind and accompanied by his grandson who provided his 'eyes'; Denis Compton, Peter May, Bill Edrich, Godfrey Evans and, most memorably, Bill Voce, who sat alongside David for much of the journey. David shared the former Nottinghamshire paceman's mining background and was both fascinated and privileged to listen to the older man's tales, particularly of the infamous Bodyline tour of 1932-33 when Voce and his partner Harold Larwood helped Douglas Jardine's team to a controversial series win.

Duncan and David stopped off in Sydney to see a business associate before moving on to join the rest of the party. The agent was based in a huge retail warehouse stacked with cricket equipment and, more surprisingly, a large selection of guns. David had developed an interest in game shooting and was impressed by a much-prized over-under Baikal shotgun with a £200 price tag. He was keen to purchase it and take it back to England but realised there would be difficulties

The Derrick Robins touring party of 1975/76.
Standing: Andrew Kennedy, Geoff Cope, Phil Carrick, John Douglas, Gary Troup, Mike Hendrick, Geoff Howarth, Dav Whatmore, Roger Tolchard. Seated: Peter Lee, David Steele, Don Bennett (asst manager), Derrick Robins, Ken Barrington (manager), David Lloyd, Frank Hayes. Front: Phil Slocombe, Trevor Chappell, Derek Randall.

Australia-bound with Duncan Fearnley.

transporting it through customs. He persuaded Duncan to assist him with his plan which was tested on the internal flight to Melbourne. Parts of the gun were separated and secreted in their luggage, David taking the stock and Duncan the barrel, and no checks were made. The journey back to England awaited.

The party gathered in the Old Bar at the Melbourne Cricket Ground on the opening day of the Centenary Test where David renewed his acquaintance with Jack Ikin, his old Staffordshire captain and a member of the England touring party to Australia under Wally Hammond's captaincy in 1946-47. The highlight of the day was a visit to Keith Miller's room in the pavilion where the Aussie swashbuckler and former fighter pilot ('pressure is a Messerschmitt up your arse') was entertaining Ikin's Lancashire teammate Brian Statham and the great Harold Larwood. David just sat, awe-struck, listening to the conversation before whispering to Duncan that 'there's plenty would like to be in our shoes now'.

Another fast bowler who had terrorised the Aussies in their own backyard was the former Northamptonshire man Frank 'Typhoon' Tyson who had taken 525 wickets at an average of 20.95 during his eight years at Wantage Road. Like David, he had played as a part-time professional in the North Staffordshire League before being enticed to Northampton by the persuasive Jock Livingston, a stylish Australian batsman who had joined the county's staff in 1950 and became the club's chief recruiter. The two found plenty to talk about during the first day's play as the hosts struggled to an unimpressive total of 138. England fared even worse in reply, dismissed for a paltry 95, and when Australia extended their lead to an apparently unassailable 462, humiliation loomed.

During England's second innings, David was enjoying Derek Randall's timely knock of 174, which helped the tourists reduce the eventual margin of defeat to a more respectable 45 runs – famously, the same result as in the very first Test match at Melbourne in 1877 – when he spotted the unmistakable blond head of a former teammate in the crowd far below him.

'Hey, Murch!' he shouted. The tanned figure turned round and replied, in his inimitable drawl, 'Steeley. How're you doin?'

It was a short conversation restricted to pleasantries and enquiries about sheep, but evoked memories of the handsome Aussie's brief spell at Wantage Road during the summer of 1968.

Stewart Nigel Clifford Murch, the son of a wealthy sheep farmer from Warrnambool, had arrived at Northampton on the recommendation of Frank Tyson, who had emigrated down under following his retirement in 1960. The flamboyant newcomer was no shrinking violet even by Australian standards and quickly began to upset the club's traditionalists. David, however, loved Murch's unconventional style, although the cavalier approach to the game was at odds with his own extreme level of dedication. No one was spared the rough end of his tongue. Whilst fielding in a second XI match, where he spent most of his time chatting up girls on the boundary, he bawled across at his captain Dennis Brookes: 'Hey Brooky, give me the ball. I'll bowl 'em out!' Even the mild-mannered and gentlemanly Brookes was sufficiently annoyed to let slip a rare expletive. One regular target for Murch's mockery was the reserved and ultra-professional Brian Reynolds.

'Hey Waddy,' he asked, pointing to his Northamptonshire capped player's tie, one of the Kettering man's most prized possessions, 'what's that bit of rag around your neck?' The perceived insult to his beloved county rankled with Brian who failed to find anything remotely amusing in the remark.

But the most common source of Murch's banter was Albert Lightfoot's over-sized proboscis.

'Jeez, Alb, but what a big hooter you've got!' he'd shout across the dressing room. 'You look like a flying wombat!'

Murch made little impression on the field of play as his first-class bowling figures reveal: one lower-order wicket for 102 on his only appearance, against Cambridge University. Indeed, his county epitaph might read: 'Did better with the girls than he did with the ball.' Towards the end of the season he discussed his prospects with Ken Turner. 'Hey Sec, what's the form next year?'

The Secretary was no fan of the Aussie show pony and didn't mince his words. 'As far as I'm concerned you could have caught yesterday's plane home. Bye bye.'

On his return to Australia, Murch enjoyed some success in state cricket for Victoria but will, for David, always be remembered for the breath of fresh Antipodean air he brought to Northampton during that single summer.

An Australian who did make a lasting impression at Wantage Road was the incomparable George Tribe. A left-arm wrist spinner and middle-order batsman, he achieved the seasonal double of 100 wickets and 1,000 runs seven times in his eight seasons at the club between 1952 and 1959. He fell short only in the wet summer of 1958 when runs were at a premium. Noted for his googlies, he also bowled the most mystifying chinaman since Ellis Achong, the West Indian Test player of Chinese descent who supposedly gave rise to the term. David had long coveted a meeting with Tribe, whose record and reputation at Northampton had been a source of fascination for many years, but when their paths eventually met it was at Melbourne airport on the day of departure. Sadly, after the briefest of introductions there was barely time for a handshake before the pair separated to catch their respective flights.

With the Baikal safely stowed in two bags the journey home was uneventful, customs were safely negotiated in that security-light era and, in the sanctity of the Heathrow car park, stock and barrel were re-united.

*

In March 1981 there was a return to southern Africa when vacancies occurred in a Leicestershire team bound for the newly created state of Zimbabwe. David joined the squad for an itinerary that included matches in Harare and Bulawayo. It was a memorable trip with numerous highlights, most notably strolling down the lawns at the back of the hotel to overlook the spectacular Victoria Falls. But

A Leicestershire lad: David joins the Foxes in Zimbabwe.
Back: Russell Cobb, David Wenlock, Nick Cook, Jonathan Agnew, Les Taylor, Gordon Parsons, John Hampshire, Peter Booth.
Front: David Steele, Grant Forster, Roger Tolchard, D Tebbutt (manager), Chris Balderstone, Tim Boon, Nigel Briers.

there was also the decidedly uncomfortable moment when he was introduced to the country's new Prime Minister, Robert Mugabe. David recalls, 'He had a handshake like a wet fish and I felt like throwing it back.'

As ever, cricket was always at the forefront of David's mind and he enjoyed pitting his wits against Zimbabwe's best, including the competitive Andy Flower and pugnacious Duncan Fletcher – both future England coaches – plus a Northamptonshire captain in years to come, Kevin Curran. Perhaps he was reflecting on losing his wicket twice to Fletcher in Bulawayo when his hotel roommate, the Yorkshire stalwart and fellow interloper John Hampshire, announced his intention to ring home. Realising that he hadn't contacted Carol for some time, David asked John to tell his wife to ring Mrs Steele and assure her that he was alright. 'I know you're a tight bugger,' Hampshire replied, 'but that takes the biscuit.'

Among the younger members of the Leicestershire squad was a twenty-year-old promising bowler named Jonathan Agnew. Writing thirty three years later in *Cricket: A Modern Anthology*, he expressed fond memories of his early acquaintance with the veteran all-rounder during the tour and offers an insightful assessment of David's character and personality:

> From the distance of the boundary edge and, indeed, on television, Steele appeared to be a dour and dull individual with more than a passing resemblance to a bespectacled middle-aged bank manager rather than an international sportsman. But when he came as a guest player on Leicestershire's tour of Zimbabwe in 1981 he was a revelation. I have yet to encounter a drier or more laconic wit ... Between making us laugh a lot, Steele also demonstrated to the Leicester lads what can be achieved by sheer hard work and dedication. He was not the most talented batsman in the world but practised relentlessly, pushed himself and was extremely brave against fast bowling ... Bowling at Steele in Championship cricket was one of the great challenges of the 1980's. Planting his front foot down the pitch, but quick to swivel onto his right foot and pull short-pitched deliveries, gave him a solid technique against fast bowling. Like many of the old-school he preferred a cap to a

helmet. I suppose he was, in a way, like a rather more humorous version of Geoffrey Boycott.

Recalling the young bowler's presence on the tour, David remembers turning a throwaway comment to his advantage. Agnew was toiling under the hot sun Salisbury sun and, while pausing to mop his sweaty brow, remarked to David, who was fielding at mid-off, 'This fast bowling's hard work. I wished I'd stayed at home with dad on our Stamford turkey farm.'

In early December the following year Carol and David were discussing purchasing the Christmas roast when Jonathan's words flooded into his mind. 'Ring directory enquiries and get a number for Agnew's turkey farm in Stamford,' he said. 'We'll be on a good thing there.' The number was obtained and David explained his credentials to an extremely affable and accommodating Agnew senior.

'Would you like a bird?' the farmer asked.

'I most certainly would,' was the reply.

'Then there's one waiting for you. Roger Tolchard [the Leicestershire wicketkeeper] has just collected his.'

David arranged to collect a prime bird at a very reasonable discount and continued the practice for several years to come.

Another memorable trip occurred in 1983 when David received an invitation to play for an International XI in Bishan Bedi's benefit match in Delhi. Having received no information regarding his hotel booking, on arriving at the airport he discovered that no one was there to meet him, least of all the host himself. With increasing anxiety, David began to ask staff and passers by if they knew of Bedi's whereabouts. Such was the great bowler's fame that it appeared everyone was familiar with the name, but no one was privy to his movements. Time passed, and David filled the waiting minutes by retrieving a bat from his luggage and playing an impromptu game with a group of cricket-mad youths who recognised him amongst the crowd in the airport concourse. At last he received word that Bishan was 'sleeping at his cousin's house', but that he was to take a cab to the Taj Palace Hotel where he was to share a room with the Pakistani

Bishan Bedi, whose benefit match gave David a chance to play alongside Holding, Lillee and Miandad.

Test player Asif Iqbal. In the hotel reception David met two other teammates, Australians Dennis Lillee and Bruce Yardley, who also queried the absence of their host. 'I haven't seen the turbaned man yet. Where is he?'

It was several days before Bedi made his appearance, standing at the top of a staircase in the hotel, resplendent in his trademark headgear, looking every inch 'the Prince'.

The match itself, between the full Indian Test team and the team of international stars which also included its captain Mushtaq Mohammad, Michael Holding, Dennis Lillee, Joel Garner and Javed Miandad, attracted a crowd of 30,000 at the city's Nehru Stadium and gave David a belated opportunity to perform on the sub-continent. He enjoyed playing in such exalted company and still relishes the sharp slip catch that dismissed Sunil Gavaskar off the bowling of 'Whispering Death' himself, Michael Holding. It was also satisfying to indulge in the high-fives celebration that he'd witnessed so often from the other side. What would Stan Crump have thought? Memories linger, but a more tangible reminder came in the form of a carpet, Bedi's gift to all participants and still much prized by the Steele household.

By the 1990s David's life had taken a more leisurely course. When he and Carol were invited to join Bob Taylor, Bob Willis, Derek

Randall, Geoff Miller and their wives on a three-week P&O cruise to the West Indies, he was delighted to accept. The cricketers' duties largely involved chatting to passengers, swapping stories and leading coaching sessions at the specially constructed nets on board.

The pleasurable experience was repeated on several occasions but most memorable was the time 'Fiery' Fred Trueman and wife, Veronica, joined the party. He announced his presence in typically bombastic style. The players had expressed their dissatisfaction at the quality of cabin accommodation provided with Fred the loudest complainant. 'My shit-house is bigger than this!' he roared at the unfortunate crew member charged with addressing the problem. 'Find us something better or we're getting off.'

His charm offensive worked and upgrades were arranged. Shortly after moving to their new cabin, David and Carol answered a loud knocking on the door to discover Fred, pipe in mouth, ready for inspection.

'You've done us well here, mate,' David remarked. 'Thanks a lot.'

Surveying the interior, the legendary bowler restricted himself to one gruff observation.

'Forty pairs,' he growled, scanning Carol's impressive collection of footwear. 'Looks like a bloody shoe shop.'

And he left.

David's first meeting with Trueman had taken place at Sheffield's Bramall Lane ground in 1964. Entering the Northamptonshire dressing room, he was surprised to see the Yorkshireman holding court and apologised for interrupting. Fred had been waiting for him.

'I've just popped in to greet you,' he said. 'You're new aren't you? Are you a batter? I'll let you have one.'

Captain Keith Andrew's arrival and sharp words soon sent Trueman packing. He was all too familiar with Fred's underhand tactics. To David's credit, if he felt intimidated he didn't show it. He survived the inevitable onslaught scoring 46 and 47 not out, earning the great bowler's grudging respect.

That quality was in short supply during the second innings when captain Brian Close decided to bring himself on for a tiring Trueman. 'Thanks, Fred,' he said. 'I'll have a go myself now.'

The bowler looked across at David and proclaimed, 'You're alright now Steeley, he can't bowl,' before launching into a stream of abuse hurled in his skipper's direction. This continued with increasing vehemence until the next batsman, Peter Watts, brother of Jim, faced four balls from Close before hitting the fifth, a long hop, straight down fine-leg's throat.

'Oh well bowled, Brian!'

Fred's rapid change of tune resonated around the ground, causing David to shake his head in disbelief. 'You two-faced bugger, Fred,' he remarked.

As he made very clear, Trueman wasn't part of the 'coaching' team on the cruise, describing his role as 'cabaret'. His agent had arranged for him to join the other more established entertainers on the ship, Jack Parnell's Dance Band, including jazz giants Kenny Baker, Don Lusher and Pat Wilcox, and the avuncular Henry Sandon of *Antiques Roadshow* fame.

Finding Fred installed in the cricketers' lounge surrounded by CDs, bats and other merchandising material, David asked who the beneficiary was.

'Charity,' was the straight-faced reply.

'Begins at home, does it?' David persisted.

'Sailors in need,' the bowler retorted, tongue firmly in cheek.

It's only fair to report that on the occasion that Carol joined the audience for one of Fred's routines she was hugely impressed. 'He just sat in a chair and told stories,' she recalled, 'but the tears were rolling down my cheeks. A very funny man.'

'And a very great bowler,' David added.

13

GOOD MORNING, BOYS

From his days coaching in South Africa during the 1960s, David had relished opportunities to pass on his knowledge and passion for the game to younger players. He knew the importance of developing a positive attitude to the game from his experiences as a youngster with Staffordshire, when attending Wednesday evening net practice meant travelling for an hour and a half on three different buses after a day's work. But it was worth it to spend time with seasoned old players like Stanley Crump and Bert Shardlow, legends in Staffordshire League cricket. The latter, a professional with Leek and his home town of Stone, was extremely fond of confectionary and regularly carried a bag of sweets in his flannels pocket. When bowling he'd pop one into his mouth and constantly run his fingers over the sticky residue on his tongue. After watching the veteran left-arm bowler take seven wickets in a Minor Counties match David asked him the secret of his success. He pointed to the sweet in his mouth.

'I wouldn't mind half a pound of them, then', the young pretender replied.

Such memories underpinned his tried-and-tested approach to teaching the game and by 1992, having been retired from first-class cricket for eight years and enjoying working back in the printing industry with Leicester-based Printstream, David was keen to renew his ties with the sport he loved. The company produced the Oakham School magazine and he took advantage of his business relationship to enquire of John Wills, the master-in-charge of cricket, if there was a vacancy – but was told that there was 'no requirement at the moment.' Later that year, however, he received more encouraging news from friend and former Oakham old boy Lynn Wilson, the Chairman of Northamptonshire CCC, who asked how he would like to be cricket coach at the school.

'That sounds good to me,' he replied and prepared for the obligatory vetting and interview by the Headmaster, Graham Smallbone, by taking a copy of his autobiography, *Come in Number Three*, 'just in case he didn't know who I was.'

He passed the test and began a new chapter of his life in the privileged surroundings of an English public school, reminiscent of his days at Wynberg almost thirty years earlier. At about the same time as David joined the staff, the school appointed a new groundsman, Keith Exton. With the school's blessing Keith began a three-year process of digging up the square and relaying the wickets and by the mid-1990s had produced twelve good pitches, each with bounce and pace. The experience certainly stood Keith in good stead as in 2008 he was appointed head groundsman at Glamorgan and, one year later, was preparing a wicket for an Ashes Test against Australia.

The new square greatly assisted David in developing techniques; batting improved as players adopted a more upright stance with the ball hitting higher up the bat. The satisfaction at witnessing his pupils' progress was enhanced by the sheer pleasure of working in such a delightful environment. He would arrive at the ground in Doncaster Place, park his car and, as was his habit during his playing days, walk over to the square and feel the pitch beneath his feet. The wicket was as true as it looked. He was never dismissed in the four innings he played for DS Steele's XI against the boys, successfully borrowing from his uncle Stanley Crump and those days at Sneyd: 'Coach them, and show them you can play.'

Delight in the setting was not confined to its physical features. It was populated by a number of characters who left their mark on the gritty former professional. As a boy, the aforementioned John Wills had accompanied his grandparents to watch Northamptonshire at the County Ground and derived great enjoyment from reliving memories of the days of Tribe, Tyson and Brookes with the newly appointed coach. The resident umpire, Kenneth Forsyth, had played Birmingham League cricket for Smethwick and was thrilled when David told him that his old teammates, Dennis Amiss and John Jameson, had recalled that 'he spun it'. There was a great sense of camaraderie and even the scorer, John Voss, a noted 'moaner', would shed his customary melancholia in the mellow atmosphere of the Wheatsheaf where players, masters and officials repaired after the game. It was all a far cry from Endon Secondary Modern, his own alma mater, but David proved a welcome addition to the ranks. The feeling was mutual and, as he reflects, 'over the years I was at the school I enjoyed the teaching staff very much.'

But it was a chance conversation with a stranger in the Stumps pavilion one afternoon in 1992 that began a friendship which David treasures to this day. John Blezard, a retired financier and cricket fanatic, had previously watched matches at Uppingham School but had felt ill at ease and decided to switch his allegiance to Oakham. David immediately felt comfortable in his presence, warming to the elderly man's charming personality and deep-rooted love of the game. John, a natural storyteller, was quickly accepted by the Oakham entourage and enjoyed holding court at one end of the bar in the Wheatsheaf while David entertained at the other. He was then driven home to Stamford. When the team was playing away, David called at the house to pick him up, enjoying a cup of tea served by John's wife Bronwen in china teacups.

'I was hugely impressed,' David recalls. 'A Staffordshire man appreciates good china.'

Their relationship bore unexpected fruit when John's son David, a retired banker, made a most generous donation to the school. Determined that his father should watch good cricket, David Blezard awarded scholarships to five boys over twelve years at great financial cost. The list of recipients makes interesting reading: Bhargav

David shares a few tips with John Blezard and two Oakham youngsters.

Modha, Yassar Tariq, Josh Cobb, Tom Fell and James Ilott. By 2009, Modha was at the Cambridge University Centre of Cricketing Excellence, Tariq was playing in the Nottinghamshire second XI, Ilott for Middlesex seconds while Cobb has become an established county player with Leicestershire and Northamptonshire. When Tom Fell arrived at the school to be assessed, David had the opportunity to vet the new scholar.

'I saw the Stafford knot on his sweater,' he recalls, 'and knew he had a chance.'

Regarded by coaches as Oakham's best-ever batsman, in recent years Fell has overcome serious illness and is now realising his early potential in Worcestershire's Championship side.

The summer of 2000 proved momentous in the sporting annals of Oakham School. The wickets were now of a high enough quality to enable first-class cricket to return for the first time since 1938 when the school played host to a Championship match between Leicestershire and Surrey. One player who found the fast, bouncy pitch to his liking was the visitors' opening batsman, Alistair Brown, who amassed a phenomenal 295 not out. Another beneficiary was the legendary Sachin Tendulkar, who appeared alongside former Northamptonshire player, Anil Kumble, when the Indian tourists played a friendly match on the ground. One shot from the little magician's wand was struck with such power that it hit the wall of the indoor school one hundred yards away.

Even more significant was the appointment to the school staff of a new physics master and director of cricket. The former Lancashire and England batsman, Frank Hayes, had worked in a coaching capacity at Felsted School where he had nurtured the development of such prominent sportsmen as Derek Pringle. Like David, he found the school to be beautifully appointed, the cricketing facilities excellent and the interviews unconventional.

As he recalls, 'Ultimately it was the Headmaster who cemented the move. Arriving late, the imposing man, who later became Headmaster of Eton College, invited me to his office and hanging up his coat addressed me with the immortal words, "I do apologise, I'm seven and a half minutes late but the claret was magnificent." I would have accepted the job for those words alone.'

Frank's imminent arrival caused David no little anxiety and he rang to express concern that his position was now in considerable jeopardy. There are semantic differences in their recollection of words spoken during that initial exchange, David opting for the more genteel, 'Does it mean I'm moving on?' while Frank remembers a more earthy response. The new appointee was quick to allay those fears, explaining that his first stipulation on obtaining the post was that David Steele would remain as the cricket professional at Oakham School forever. It was the beginning of a coaching partnership which, in Frank's words, 'was to become one of the most fruitful, certainly in the history of Oakham, but possibly nationwide as well.'

The relationship was founded on mutual respect. The pair had each scored Test centuries against the fearsome West Indian pace attack during the 1970s and, as a member of the successful Lancashire side of that period, Frank had witnessed David's dogged determination to score runs against one of the best county bowling attacks in the country. His courage in playing the quicks, his mastery of spin, his wily bowling and remarkable catching ability earned Hayes' grudging admiration but these qualities were not always appreciated by some of his red rose teammates. In Frank's words, 'He didn't drink and he certainly didn't buy!' David's alleged parsimony was not restricted to his pocket, causing the England fast bowler Ken Shuttleworth to hate him with a real relish. As Frank recalls, 'When Steeley arrived at the crease with the air of a swindling bank clerk, Ken's hackles were up. But he couldn't get him out. Faster and faster though he bowled he still couldn't get him out and – to add insult to injury – he played him off the front foot!'

But there was a different side to the unsmiling, dour character who occupied the wicket, as Frank discovered when accompanying David in Derrick Robins' touring side to South Africa early in 1976. Away from the field of play he became privy to the dry wit, the wry observations and his profound thoughts on the game which he obviously loved with a passion. The roots of their partnership were established then as they discovered a mutual belief in the principles that would guide their approach to teaching the game. As Hayes recalls, 'We were both extremely suspicious of any sort of coaching from the book and the boys quickly appreciated the pair of us did not believe in baffling young players with the ever encroaching sports science but, instead, concentrated on enhancing their own natural style and ability. Expressing oneself on the pitch was imperative and the great game was to be enjoyed to the fullest.'

The traditional but rapidly becoming unorthodox approach soon paid off. Eton were beaten in their first game with Oakham after David had informed the opposition master-in-charge, Mr Ralph Oliphant-Callum, that the sides, 'would play only a *proper* game of declaration cricket and not the rotten game of limited overs that he was proposing.'

Frank Hayes retains affectionate memories of the day Harrow were thrashed on their own patch. 'The scene was set when, straight off the minibus, the seasoned old pro handed the captain a box of balls instructing him to give the team some fielding practice, stressing also, in no uncertain manner, that he would put the opposition in on a wicket he described as "green as old boots". He and I then viewed proceedings from the pavilion while sipping a pleasant cup of Yorkshire tea. The Oakham boys were in charge, whereas the Harrow team was drilled into the ground by three separate cricket coaches.'

Not only did the pair have a similar approach to the technical part of the game but their personalities also complemented each other. Frank was a gifted teacher, familiar with the psychology of successfully motivating pupils in the classroom, while David spared no one with his often blunt, no-nonsense attitude. As Hayes recalls 'He was made of stern stuff, hewn, like his dad, out of the toughest Staffordshire coal. He backed his own intuitive judgement, whether at odds or not with those around him.'

The unbeaten 2003 Oakham side with Frank Hayes (back left) and David (back right). Seated furthest left is Oakham's most famous cricket alumnus, Stuart Broad.

He remembers a lunch interval with players, coaches and staff happily enjoying the school's fabled hospitality, when his fellow coach was regaling the company with a lengthy tale about Colin Milburn, glass of wine in hand. To David's great annoyance a rather gangling fast bowler had the temerity to interrupt, proclaiming that he had hurt his leg and needed to go straight to the medical centre for attention.

'Go down there,' the professional said, 'and you'll not get out for a week.'

The injured bowler rolled up his trousers to reveal an egg- shaped bruise on his leg. But this gesture merely compounded his mistake.

Steeley, desperate to get back to his story, retorted with some disdain, 'Injured? You'll bowl that off! Now run along and don't let me find you down that bloody medical centre.'

To the consternation of the opposition master-in-charge and the rest of the gathering, David quickly returned to his story, having little truck with the new era of health and safety.

On the resumption of play after lunch, the self-same lad ran in and demolished the opposition with a spell of three wickets for 9 runs helping secure Oakham's comfortable victory. After the match, as the boy received congratulations for his devastating spell, David invited him to roll up his trouser leg. Sure enough, the egg-shaped lump had disappeared.

Praise had to be earned, and excuses were never tolerated. When Tom Fell complained about having to practise on a green, damp wicket, David referred to facing Higgs and Statham in their pomp bowling on a far wetter one. He told him to move his feet, get to the pitch of the ball or get right back on his stumps and assured him that if he could play on that he could play on anything.

Another prospect, Josh Cobb, was on the receiving end of a tongue-lashing when falling for thirty in a festival match against Wellington School. David had spent hours working with the boy on his technique in the nets and had been delighted with his progress so was incandescent when he learned of his dismissal hitting a full-toss straight to deep mid-off. Whether it was the memory of Len Hutton's advice to the callow Colin Cowdrey during that distant tour of Australia, the fact that his own advice had been so wilfully disregarded or, more likely, the batsman's attempt to exonerate himself by unduly crediting the bowler, David was unsparing in his criticism.

'Another bloody thirty,' he said, 'while that bastard from Sedburgh got 168 yesterday. I played some bloody shots in my time but if I'd played one like that, I wouldn't have gone home for a week. My cat would have done better than that. That's the last time I bowl *you* any rotten balls.'

As Frank Hayes recalls, 'It was certainly not in Steeley's domain to mince words and the listening parents' faces painted a picture to behold. But that's the way it was and we both believed that it was a cardinal sin to lie to yourself and make excuses. It was a lesson that young people had to learn, accept your failings and move on.'

That evening the unfortunate Cobb and the rest of the team sat down with the two coaches for a beer while trading stories about the great game. Much was gleaned about all aspects of life and cricket and it's likely that Josh Cobb, now one of the country's outstanding one-day players and a great ambassador for Oakham School, has never forgotten that innings, the shot he played, and his mentor's severe dressing down.

David never shirked his responsibility when it came to parents, detesting those who mollycoddled their sons or adversely coached them. Some, like the England and Nottinghamshire batsman, Chris Broad, allowed the coaches free rein from which son Stuart clearly benefited. Others were suffocating in their over-protectiveness. 'Let them breathe!' David urged.

One of the worst offenders in David's eyes was another former England player, the Essex fast bowler Neil Foster. Having been on the receiving end of a private dressing-down from Frank Hayes for video-ing his son batting during an early season game, Neil had stayed away from subsequent matches until Oakham played at Stowe. When David spotted him setting up his tripod on the deep cover boundary as Henry Foster approached the wicket and took guard, he was furious.

His anger intensified when the young batsman was out first ball, and he strode round the outfield to berate the unfortunate parent.

'Who the hell are you? David Attenborough? Take that contraption down before I throw it in the rhododendron bushes. You just got him out. He looked at the camera, not the ball.'

Henry handled the situation well when David spoke to his pupil later that day, making sure his father clearly understood the coach's message: 'All cameras banned!'

Later that season, coach and parent met again at a match at Eton where David couldn't resist a quick quip. 'It's not in your bag?' he asked, with that characteristic wry smile.

Despite his hard-bitten approach to discipline and commitment, David had a softer edge when addressing the specific needs of individual players. As Frank Hayes recounts, his approach paid scant homage to political correctness but could be hugely effective.

> On one occasion we were discussing the plight of a gifted but over-weight aspiring young cricketer who could just not get to catches and was rarely able to bowl more than a few overs of fast medium seam without a break. When, referring to him as Billy, after the infamous Greyfriars character, I suggested that he seemed to be bowling respectable slow left-arm in the far net, David was gone in a flash.
>
> 'Billy,' he said to the corpulent bowler, 'a word please.'
>
> 'My name's not Billy, Sir,' replied the unfortunate boy.
>
> 'Well you look like him, lad.' David continued, although the pupil had no idea at all who Billy Bunter was. 'How about bowling left-arm spin instead of that quick rubbish? Likely you'll be able to bowl a few more overs.'
>
> He then worked with him in the nets for two hours before wishing him goodbye.
>
> 'Well done, Billy. We'll make a cricketer of you yet. And, Billy, go easy on those pies.'
>
> The boy went away in astonishment but, that year, took twenty wickets for the first XI bowling left-arm spin. He's now playing for a Premier League side, batting at number four, turning his arm over to good effect, has never forgotten his time at Oakham and is still as big as a barrel.

The Hayes/Steele partnership ended in 2008 but had coincided with a golden era in the school's sporting history. During that time seven former Oakhamians made their mark on the professional game, with Stuart Broad the greatest of them all.

As a promising but raw youngster, even Stuart did not escape the rough end of David's tongue. After one particularly unimpressive net session he was told, 'I don't care what they're telling you down the county, you don't bowl that rubbish when you play for Oakham. You pitch it up and hit the top of off-stump.'

The advice paid off handsomely, young Broad ending his four-year first-XI career with sixty-one wickets at 23.34 and 902 runs at 37.58. His cricketing apprenticeship successfully completed, he joined Leicestershire and began the journey that would lead to recognition as one of England's finest pace bowlers who could bat a bit too.

In 2015 Stuart Broad submitted an article to the *Times Educational Supplement* in which he identified his most influential teachers as Frank Hayes and David Steele. He pays tribute to Frank, 'a great

Master and pupil: Staurt Broad and David reunite at an England Players' dinner, with Roy Swetman, Joe Root and John Snow.

storyteller, whose innovative, practical approach to teaching made science lessons exciting. This simplistic, uncomplicated methodology extended to his cricket coaching with its emphasis on basic skills and has underpinned Stuart's attitude as a professional player.'

Of Frank's coaching partner he says: 'David was different. He was pure cricket. He is a huge character and does the best after-dinner speaking there is. He has made a career out of it now but back then he was superb at firing our enthusiasm by talking and telling stories. You would stroll around the boundary with him and he would tell you about the past, about how he used to face the Australians, and it just made you want to play. They worked rather well as a duo. Frank was more serious than David, who was relaxed about absolutely everything. You would rarely find him in a bad mood, apart from when people were late – that was an absolute no-no, something that has stuck with me throughout my career. Frank was probably a bit more direct in his coaching – he would get you in the nets and would work on different techniques, but David was all about the theatre of cricket. The majesty. The excitement. For both of them, I guess it came down to storytelling. Kids love stories. It's not exactly revolutionary.'

Surprisingly, Stuart seems to have overlooked David's emphasis on the importance of nets in developing his range of cricketing skills, an approach cultivated during those early days spent in Uncle Stan's backyard or the nets at Sneyd. But those unsolicited words of praise are sincere and a source of great pride.

14

Home truths

David's elder son Arran was born in January 1975 and Mark followed almost two years later. Reflecting upon growing up in the Steele household, they recognise the traditional roles played by their parents. Carol was the homemaker, David the breadwinner. During the summer he went off to cricket and for the rest of the year immersed himself in his work as a sales executive in the print trade. Carol, meanwhile, fulfilled her domestic duties, enjoying ministering to the needs of her children and wider family. This included David's father Alf who, in his declining years, moved into a cottage in Geddington just a few doors away.

The boys recall their visits to their grandfather with some amusement: 'He was nothing like Dad. He wasn't the most welcoming of people, shunned new acquaintances and was a bit odd. His strict Methodist upbringing and hard working life contributed to his austere, rather cold demeanour. If you dared ask for a sweet too early in the visit he'd bellow, "Wait for the Polo!" In honesty, we were a little scared of him and occasionally took refuge behind the sofa. Curiously, when making up the fire he used just ten pieces of coal and when we asked why, he'd say, "If you had to go underground to get it, there'd be plenty of gas fires about!"'

In his autobiography *Come in Number Three,* published in 1977, David ruminated upon the boys' futures as possible professional cricketers: 'If they want to go into the game then I will be delighted, although I'll do as my own parents did with John and myself and make sure they have another career behind them first. I'm not going to say I won't ram cricket down their throats, because I will, just in the same way it happened to me, but I will not be pushing too hard because that is the way to kill the interest completely.'

He soon made his intentions clear. Each was presented with a miniature bat while still in the pram and cricketing analogies formed part of their early language development. A concrete wicket, reminiscent of the strip in Uncle Stanley's Chell Green backyard, was laid in the spacious garden and the boys 'got stuck in'. As Arran recalls, 'We both loved cricket and spent inordinate amounts of time playing, listening and talking about the game with Dad, who was a great sounding board and mentor.'

Both Arran and Mark were talented cricketers but neither made their careers in the first-class game. Arran moved from the local village school to Oundle where his first day coincided with that of John Wake, a newly appointed master and teammate of David's in the Bedfordshire side. After captaining Northamptonshire U19s at the

Baby Arran joins David in the dressing room during the 1975 Ashes.

annual Cambridge Festival in 1994, he went on to gain a degree in Psychology at Newcastle University where he played for the first XI. In 1998 there were appearances for Somerset, Nottinghamshire and Durham seconds before work, marriage and children brought his playing career to an early end. His only List A appearance was in 1999 when he represented the Northamptonshire Cricket Board in a NatWest Trophy match against Wiltshire, scoring 23.

Brother Mark went to Wellingborough School and was fortunate to experience the relaxed approach of another of his father's former colleagues, the redoubtable John Dye. Under the Doc's tutelage Mark enjoyed great success and played in an English Schools trial game during which he removed a future England captain, a certain Andrew Flintoff. From the age of ten he and Arran had also enjoyed happy and productive seasons with the Northamptonshire Cricket Association, managed by Peter O'Toole's favourite coach, John Malfait. When Oundle and Wellingborough schools played each other for the first time in many years, Arran and Mark lined up on opposing sides!

One of the most pleasant venues the boys and their parents visited was Everdon Hall, home of cricketing connoisseur Captain Dick Hawkins. The ground with its picturesque thatched pavilion was founded in 1899 by his father, Henry, a former Northamptonshire player, and hosted countless matches over the years. A great supporter of youth cricket and a firm believer in promoting local youngsters, Captain Hawkins was delighted to stage NCA fixtures, several of which involved the junior Steeles. After watching Mark hit an unbeaten fifty against Hampshire he remarked, 'That's what I like to see. Like father, like son.' And Mark still owes a debt to Malfait: 'He was utterly committed and made great sacrifices to give we lads – including future county players Mal Loye, the Swann brothers, Alec and Graeme, and Kevin Innes – wonderful opportunities to develop our games. During winter weekends he'd drive us all down to Lord's for net practice.'

After completing his studies at Kettering's Tresham College, Mark joined the playing staff at Northamptonshire, a decision that still causes David much regret. 'With hindsight, he should have taken the opportunity afforded as an MCC Young Cricketer and gone down to Lord's, where he'd have been looked after much better.'

There is little doubt that Mark failed to achieve his full potential at Wantage Road. David had always stressed his beliefs that 'you've got to do it for yourself' and that 'cream comes to the top', expecting that Mark's natural ability would shine through in the end.

Arran is more pragmatic. 'That might be true for a genius, but everyone else requires luck, timing, support and a mentor. This was sadly lacking at Northamptonshire County Cricket Club at that time and Mark suffered accordingly.'

Looking back, Mark ponders philosophically on what proved an unhappy time at the County Ground.

'I was too young and never really had the chance to establish myself either as a batsman or a bowler. I remember one game for the county colts against Peterborough in the Northants League when my immaturity was all too evident. I was bowling to their Cambridgeshire all-rounder, the talented Ajaz Akhtar, and so intent on creating a good impression that I tried too hard. He dug out the first

Mark (front right) receives a Lord's Taverners award alongside Mal Loye (back right) and Kevin Innes (left) in 1990.

ball and hit it straight into the West Stand where my father, of all people, was sitting! The next two balls received similar treatment, the over eventually costing 24 runs. As Dad likes to recall, a chap walked past and asked him, "Who the bloody hell's bowling here?" "I haven't a clue," he replied with a straight face. "He's useless, get him off."'

Good humoured banter has always been a feature of the boys' relationship with their father, who can never resist the quick quip. After taking four wickets for Northamptonshire seconds against Middlesex, Mark rang David with the news.

'Well done, youth,' he replied.

'They included a hat-trick, Dad.'

'Never. You've got to bowl three balls straight for that.'

Mark eventually left Northamptonshire and joined Derbyshire, making a number of appearances in the second XI. One was at Chesterfield against a Yorkshire side which included England Test players Ryan Sidebottom and Matthew Hoggard. After the former had beaten the outside edge of the bat on numerous occasions, he shouted down the wicket to the fortunate batsman, 'Hey Steeley, you may not have inherited your father's genes but you certainly got your mother's.'

It was a short-lived move to David's old stamping ground that fully restored Mark's love of the game. In 1998 he made ten appearances for Staffordshire in its Minor Counties Championship-winning side, batting at six, bowled regularly, and took two for 43 in his only List A game against Leicestershire in the NatWest Trophy.

The Steele family radiates warmth with David at its core. No grandchild need feel uncomfortable in *his* presence as he plays the doting grandad to a tee. His unpretentious, humorous good nature attracts a wide circle of friends from across social borders. He's never happier than while discussing cricket and so, as Arran and Mark are often reminded, are many of their business contacts. Neither seeks to play the 'Steele' card but, should the close family link emerge naturally in conversation, clients are quick to recall their favourite memories of the bank clerk who went to war.

PART FOUR

EMBOSSING

15

Catches win matches

David's game involved batting, bowling and fielding. The first two elements required constant practice, but catching came naturally. Keith Andrew, David's first captain at Northamptonshire, quickly recognised this ability and gave him free rein to occupy the area from leg slip to short leg depending upon the bowler. For David Larter or Brian Crump it was the former, while the bouncy spin of Haydn Sully, Mushtaq Mohammed and Bishan Bedi brought him closer to the bat.

The importance of holding on to the slightest chance was brought home in a game against Gloucestershire at Northampton in May 1966. Play had begun late on a rain-affected wicket and Northamptonshire managed just 72. The opposition's openers, Arthur Milton and Ron Nicholls, had three-quarters of an hour to bat before close of play, which on that occasion was seven o'clock. It was important to achieve an early breakthrough which duly came when Nicholls unexpectedly glanced a ball from Larter to leg. It flew towards David's right hand, he dived full-length and caught it, putting the opposition a vital man down before a run had been scored. 'That's a bonus,' Larter exclaimed. 'It didn't feel like a wicket ball.'

Nicholls' dismissal heralded a procession back to the pavilion as Brian Crump bagged six for 14 in Gloucestershire's even more dismal

David Larter, who benefited from a David Steele catch on sixteen occasions.

response: all out for 66. Sadly, the Northamptonshire second innings showed only a slight improvement and, after Keith Andrew's generous declaration, their opponents crept home by one wicket.

Larter wasn't the only bowler to express his gratitude to the catcher. As the great Mushtaq was wont to say when praised for his wicket-taking prowess, 'Steeley caught 'em.' An example of this effective combination came during a match between Leicestershire and Northamptonshire in July 1972 with the brothers Steele in opposition. John was well on the way to a hard-earned century when, on 91, he swept Mushtaq towards the square-leg boundary. He got a top edge but felt the ball would drop safely just past the square leg umpire and completed the first run quickly before turning to check the possibility of a second. To his surprise he saw David had left his customary position at backward short leg and was running at full speed before diving to catch the ball at full stretch with his reliable

John Steele
Benefit
Year 1983

David's brother, John, was also an excellent catcher. He played for Liecestershire for fourteen seasons, being granted a benefit in the last, before ending his career at Glamorgan.

left hand. In conversation later John suggested to his brother that it was really cousin Crump's catch, as he was fielding at deep square leg, to which David replied, 'I just saw the ball and went for it.'

When reflecting on the modern game, David is astounded that so little use is made of the specialist fielder, especially close to the wicket. It is a view shared by his brother who, like David, was a fine exponent of the position. When John joined Leicestershire in 1970 the captain was Ray Illingworth, a highly skilful off-spinner who, bowling on uncovered pitches at that time, was almost unplayable. Most counties had a number of specialist spinners – John was the fourth in the Leicestershire side alongside Illingworth, Jack Birkenshaw and Chris Balderstone – and the close fielder was a vital ally and integral member of the team. Like his brother, John adjusted his position depending upon conditions and the batsman's style of play. For example, he would field finer for David as he knew his tendency to push well forward with the bat in front of the pad.

The brothers understood each other's strengths and weaknesses and no quarter was shown in their rivalry on the field of play. This was exemplified during a game between Glamorgan, where John had decamped from Leicestershire at the beginning of the season, and Northamptonshire in August 1984. On the third and final day of the match he was sitting in the changing room at the lunch interval thinking about the chances of carrying his first innings return of four for 27 into the opposition's second innings.

'The door suddenly burst open and there stood the great Mr Wilf Wooller, the former Glamorgan captain, Welsh rugby international and one of the country's most lauded sportsmen. He spotted me sitting in the corner and shouted that he'd been out on the ground looking at the wicket and if I didn't get five more wickets I should be shot – in a manner of speaking. I managed four, one of which was David's. Apparently when he arrived back in the pavilion he was extremely agitated, pacing round and round the dressing room. Rob Bailey kept asking him if it was a bad decision and eventually he sat down, looked at his young teammate and said, woefully, "It's seven-six to our youth!" Winston Davis's catch off my bowling meant I'd taken his wicket seven times to his six, and he was devastated. To rub extra salt into the wound I did mention later that when he'd dismissed me in a benefit game only first-class matches counted so the final score was actually seven-five.'

The sibling competition even extended to the only occasion that the brothers lined up in the same team for a first-class match, when they were chosen to represent TN Pearce's XI against the West Indies at Scarborough in September 1973. John had opened the batting in the first innings, but in the second Ken McEwan had taken his place at the top of the order as the Essex player needed to leave early to catch a train home. John eventually walked to the wicket at 5.58 pm, just two minutes before the close of play on the final day to join David, the not-out batsman, at the crease.

'I tried to walk as slowly as possible to the middle, so that it might be the last over of the match,' John recalls. 'I was greeted by brother and asked him what the bowler, Inshan Ali, a left-arm wrist spinner, was doing with the ball. He assured me that if I played for the straight one I'd be alright. I did and was caught behind by wicket-keeper Deryck Murray, first ball. The umpires then called time. So much for brotherly love!'

David, inevitably, has a humorous take on the story. 'Back in the pavilion I said, "I'm usually better than you, John, but this time *you've* got the edge!"'

The Steele brothers were members of the large body of specialist spin bowlers and close fielders that proliferated in first-class cricket in those days. Reflecting upon the lack of such players today, John maintains, 'having been involved in the game for over forty years, I have seen their demise due to covered wickets, four-day cricket (only one spinner in the team), and a one-day mentality by captains in their field settings for the spinners.'

However, close fielding positions carried considerable risk in the days before helmets and other protective devices. To the seasoned professional cricketer in that era there was, as the old adage has it, 'no gain without pain.' During Somerset's second innings of a high-scoring Championship match against Derbyshire at Taunton in 1981, David was on the receiving end of a meaty Viv Richards shot off Iain Anderson which struck his shin, causing a swelling of golf ball proportions. Captain Barry Wood suggested he leave the field for treatment, which David was most happy to do. He'd taken nought for sixty at that point and respite from a dominant Richards on a flat batting track was much appreciated. On arriving back in the pavilion he sought attention from the Somerset physio in the absence of his Derbyshire counterpart, urging him to 'make it last for an hour to save me going for a hundred'. He probably felt he'd earned a rest having contributed handsomely to a third-wicket partnership of 291 with South African Peter Kirsten during Derbyshire's first innings.

There were many similar incidents. When fielding at short-leg to Bishan Bedi against Glamorgan at St Helen's, Swansea he was knocked to the ground by Majid Khan's powerful sweep. Wicket-keeper George Sharp's barely stifled laughter was not welcome and received short shrift from the unfortunate fielder who continued to lay prone and in considerable distress. His tribulations were noted by the Northamptonshire coach and former opening batsman Brian Reynolds from the pavilion balcony, who alerted club physio Jack Jennings.

'Steeley's down, Jack. I heard a crack.'

Jack remained glued to his copy of *Sporting Life*. He clearly resented the intrusion while assiduously studying form but was even more disturbed by the prospect of descending the 250 or so concrete steps to the playing area followed by the laborious climb back.

'Why don't you go?' he asked Reynolds, 'You're the younger man,' adding after a moment's thought, 'If he gets up he'll be alright. If he doesn't, we'll both go down.'

Back on the pitch David's teammates surrounded their stricken colleague, who had spotted the discussion on the balcony.

'Do you think either of them will come down?' he enquired anxiously.

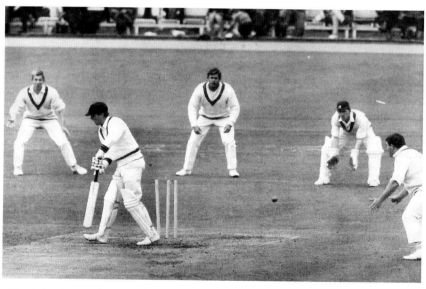

David takes a close catching position for Northamptonshire against the Australians in 1968 – but isn't needed as Paul Sheahan is bowled for a duck.

'No chance. Grin and bear it,' was the response with the inevitable palliative, 'Run it off!'

As a close catcher himself, David was appreciative of teammates who also put themselves in the firing line, reflecting that 'players of quality in close positions give bowlers a massive boost'.

He reserves particular admiration for Colin Milburn and Geoff Cook. Ollie's extra bulk belied his nimbleness and lightning reflexes which earned him forty victims in the 1964 season alone – a club record – while Cook's 375 catches put him second to DS Steele in the Northamptonshire annals. His proximity to the bat was perilous at times as recalled in an incident from a match against Middlesex at Wellingborough School when, fielding at short-leg to Peter Willey's medium cutters, he was struck on the head by a powerfully struck shot from batsman Norman Featherstone that would have been a certain boundary. Fortunately he was wearing a helmet and the ball ricocheted over wicketkeeper Sharp towards slip where Roy Virgin dived but dropped it. The bowler was incandescent.

'What are you playing at Virg?' he bellowed.

The rest of the players were more concerned about their injured colleague, who continued to lay prostrate on the floor.

'Never mind Virg, what about Cooky?' they asked.

'He'll get over it,' Willey replied, still smarting over the missed chance. 'He'll get up.'

And, of course, he did.

Dropped catches can lose matches but they can also have a major effect upon a player's career. Back in 1966, when coaching at St Andrew's School in South Africa, David had encountered fast bowler Rupert Hanley, then aged just fourteen. Nicknamed 'Spook', he joined Northamptonshire and played a number of matches in the summer of 1984. After recording the outstanding figures of six for 21 against a strong Lancashire batting side at Southport, his next game was a John Player League fixture at Wellingborough on 12 August where Worcestershire provided the opposition. Despite his undoubted prowess with the ball his fielding was decidedly weak, and when big hitter David Smith slammed bowler Steele high in the air in

Rupert 'Spook' Hanley, whose lacklustre fielding didn't endear him to all his Northamptonshire colleagues in 1984.

the direction of Rupert at long-on he showed little inclination to get under the ball. His token gesture involved feigning a tumble, dropping the ball and landing in an awkward heap on the grass, where he remained for several minutes. The incident was viewed from short-leg by captain Geoff Cook, who showed scant concern for the stricken fielder.

'Not interested in Spook's injury, Skip? David asked.

'Only if he's broken his leg,' the dour North Easterner replied, before aiming what proved a valedictory remark at the South African. 'It looks like it's the end of the war for you, Dougie!' (A pointed reference to the leg-less Second World War flier, Douglas Bader.)

Despite those heroics just days earlier against Lancashire, Hanley never played another game for Northamptonshire and, in David's words, 'was soon on the iron bird bound for Cape Town.'

Another victim of the curse of the dropped catch was revealed in a match between Derbyshire and Somerset at Taunton in September 1979. During the hosts' second innings the magnificent Viv Richards was in full flow, so much so that Geoff Miller withdrew himself from the action citing an injury – thus exposing fellow spinner Steele to the West Indian's fire and fury. As Derbyshire had no twelfth man available Somerset kindly lent one of their reserves, a certain David Gurr, once of Oxford University who had made a limited number of appearances in the county's colours. The replacement had hardly enough time to position himself on the boundary near the pavilion steps when Richards hit David hard and high in Gurr's direction. It was a real sitter which dropped straight into his hands. Sadly the ball didn't stay there, but passed through, struck him on the chest and fell to the ground. The players left the field shortly afterwards but instead of retreating to the sanctuary of the home dressing room, the unfortunate fielder remained in post waiting to proffer his apology. As David and his teammates approached, Alan Hill attempted to console the abject Gurr.

'Never mind Steeley, these things happen,' he said loudly.

The bowler was in unsympathetic mood. 'Not off this man they don't,' he replied with a gesture towards the batsman.

Richards went on to make 89. Gurr never played for Somerset again.

David's own catching proficiency was widely recognised across the county circuit. Remembering a game against Lancashire at Old Trafford in the Benson and Hedges Cup, he recalls Clive Lloyd getting a fierce top-edge off a ball from Kapil Dev which flew 'miles' into the air towards square-leg where he was fielding alongside umpire, Bill Alley.

'I'll leave it to you, Steeley,' drawled the droll Aussie.

The ball continued to steeple high above him against a cloudy sky, fortunately the best of backgrounds, before beginning to drop like a stone. He had time to remove his cap and get ready but maintained concentration, the key to the art, as he watched the ball all the way down before finally clutching it inches from the ground.

Events had been observed from the Lancashire dressing room by Jack Simmons, the next batsman in.

'Who's under it?' he asked teammate Frank Hayes, as the ball fell rapidly to earth.

'Steeley,' was the reply.

'Then I'm on my way,' he said, resigned to his fate.

The story illustrates David's remarkable catching ability, underpinned by unshakable self-belief, which brought him his 533 first-class victims.

'Wherever the ball went in the air,' he maintains, 'I wanted it.'

The figures suggest the confidence was justified.

16

FACING THE QUICKS AND OTHER CHALLENGES

'Nobody likes facing the quick bowlers, but some batters play them better than others.'

David developed much of his batting technique whilst playing in the North Staffordshire League as a youngster. The wickets were generally easy-paced, kept low, seamed and turned, and they were a vital proving ground for any aspiring batsman as there was no shortage of quick bowlers. One of the most dangerous at the time was Knypersley's professional Brian Jackson, a very effective medium-fast seamer who played for Cheshire in the Minor Counties before enjoying success in the first-class game with Derbyshire. Against such bowlers David adopted the approach which characterised his batting throughout his long career.

'I always looked to get forward. I found it quicker to get from the front to the back than the back to the front and worked very hard on my top hand to keep it straight. Playing against the quicks, I looked at them with my weight on the front foot in the stance, picking up the length of the ball in this way. As I became more experienced I didn't have any fear of facing fast bowling: the only fear was getting out.'

During his two English summers of Test cricket, David faced four of the most celebrated exponents of quick bowling in the history of the game. Each presented unique challenges.

'Dennis Lillee was probably the most comfortable to face as his smooth action sprung few surprises beyond sheer pace. Jeff Thomson was more unpredictable. He bowled from wide of the crease and had a bow-and-arrow action which made him very difficult to pick. The five overs I faced against him during the first innings of the fourth Test at The Oval in 1975 were the fastest I've ever encountered. I was actually out three times in that innings. Successive balls from Tommo bounced, left me, I got a nick and was caught behind. Fortunately both were called no balls. Dennis then got me with a yorker for 39.'

England followed on 341 runs behind on first innings with two and a half days of the six-day Test to bat and, after losing Barry Wood cheaply, John Edrich and David knuckled down in a rearguard action. They survived until the close of play on day three and resumed the following day in bright sunshine, the pitch dry, its demons departed. Together they added to their overnight scores compiling a second-wicket stand of 125 which contributed to the match-saving total of 538.

As David reflects, 'It's nice to bat well in situations that are vital There's now a lack of technique against both real pace and spin because our players don't have experience of either in county cricket and develop bad habits playing the one-day and Twenty20 stuff. You need quick feet against pace, don't show the bowler your wickets and tire them out. During the 2017/18 Test series in Australia, Alastair Cook demonstrated how to knuckle down for the really long haul and by that time the series was virtually lost anyway. Funnily enough, his double century was the second I watched him score. The first was getting on for twenty years ago when, during my time as coach, I'd taken the Oakham School team to play at Bedford. Their coach, Derek Randall, was quick to point out a young left-hander having a knock in the nets. "You'll like him, Steeley," he said. "He can play." And play he did. He scored his first hundred before lunch and his second between lunch and tea.'

Hook and you're out: David loses his wicket against the West Indies in 1976.

In the 1976 series against the West Indies, Andy Roberts' change of pace provided David with a different challenge.

'He had the ability to bowl two types of bouncer, one a yard quicker than the other. A man of few words, when I eventually managed to get an explanation of his technique from him he just said, "I jump up a bit higher." Michael Holding relied on pure speed and accuracy, delivered with the most beautifully smooth action. Standing at the non-striker's end I watched with awe as he came in to bowl and coined the phrase that became common parlance in the game: Whispering Death.'

Another West Indian, Surrey's Sylvester Clarke, proved a fearsome opponent, generally bowling round the wicket and deliberately targeting the batsman. During Northamptonshire's Championship match at The Oval in May 1984, Rob Bailey watched Clarke's hostile deliveries with trepidation and, fearing for the veteran batsman's safety, persuaded David to don a helmet for the first time in his career. When the time came to bat he reluctantly put on the helmet and made his way to the wicket to face an expectant Clarke.

> The helmet was really uncomfortable, it kept dislodging my glasses and I couldn't see properly. As I approached the square Sylvester shouted across, 'Hey Steeley, take that tin pot off your head. Don't lower yourself, you don't need that.'
>
> I decided to appeal to his good nature and replied, 'I'll take it off if you bowl me a few off-breaks.'
>
> He smiled, I removed the helmet, and he came in to bowl. The ball arrowed towards me, passed perilously close to my nose and flew through to the wicketkeeper.
>
> 'You bastard, Clarkey!' I shouted.
>
> He smiled again. 'Come on Steeley,' he said. 'Let's get down to business.'

The use of protective equipment was limited during the 1960s and the absence of an arm guard contributed to the only serious injury David suffered during his playing days. However, the bowler's contribution cannot be underestimated. The incident occurred during a Championship game against Gloucestershire at Northampton in June 1969. Gloucester were responding to Northamptonshire's first-innings total of 205 when play resumed on Monday morning after the Sunday break. Tony Durose bowled the first over of the day from the football ground end to the hard-hitting, all-action all-rounder, Mike Procter. The fourth ball pitched well outside the off stump, seamed back a foot, and knocked the South African's off-stick out of the ground. Fielding at slip, David threw his arms up in delight, but noticed Procter's angry glare in his direction as the disappointed batsman made his way back to the pavilion, dismissed for just six. Gloucester eventually declared on 365 for eight. Facing a large deficit, Northamptonshire had scored 50 for three in their second innings when David went out to bat. He recalls events with clarity.

'Procter ran in for his first ball to me, it reared off the wicket and smacked me on the front arm. I dropped the bat in pain and looked down the track to Albert Lightfoot at the other end. He came across to see if I was alright but I couldn't pick the bat up and knew I couldn't carry on. I returned to the pavilion where my uncle Stanley Crump was watching the game. He had a quick look at my arm and said, "What you need are comfrey leaves. Boil them up and wrap them around the limb and the problem will go away." I went home that evening and spent the night carrying out his advice, packing the leaves around my arm, but the pain just intensified. Next morning I went back to the ground and consulted our physio, Jack Jennings, who took me to hospital, where an x-ray confirmed I'd broken both bones in the arm. So much for comfrey leaves! What made things worse, though, was discovering that Procter had bowled a fifteen-yard ball on purpose, maintaining that he'd seen me laughing at his dismissal on Monday morning.'

Revenge of sorts was gained eight years later in a thrilling game in the second round of the Gillette Cup at Bristol in 1977. Requiring 242 to win, the Northamptonshire batsmen were subjected to a barrage of hostile bowling from Procter and were soon two wickets down. With the crowd in the Jessop Stand baying, 'Kill, kill,' David and partner Mushtaq held firm as the match went into a second day. Respite came the following morning as, with overs rationed, Procter was taken out of the attack and replaced by the more benign partnership of David Graveney and Julian Shackleton. The two batsmen made proverbial hay and amassed a competition-record-breaking stand of 140, bringing victory within clear sight. The responsibility for getting their side over the line eventually rested with bowlers Alan Hodgson and Bishan Bedi but, with eight runs required off the final over, Procter had returned to the attack. As the South African thundered for his first ball Bedi stepped back almost to square leg, hung out his bat, and got an inside edge which took the ball to the boundary.

Watching nervously from the pavilion, David shouted words of encouragement, 'Get behind it Bish!'

'You bat!' the fearful Bedi replied, holding out his blade in supplication.

'I have been,' retorted David, as the batsman prepared to face another thunderbolt.

Repeating his stance, the beleaguered Bedi got another inside edge, another four and the game was won.

One of the most significant differences between the world of professional cricket in David's era and today is in the treatment of its most important commodity: the players. Strict fitness regimes were largely unheard of and more rigorous approaches to players' physical wellbeing were often treated with disdain. When the Northamptonshire squad arrived for pre-season training on the traditionally appointed day, 1 April, in 1964 they were in for a considerable surprise. Secretary Turner introduced, in peremptory fashion, a craggy, crinkly haired figure clad in a well-worn tracksuit 'This is Mac. He's going to get you fit. Over to you, sir.' And he walked away.

Charles McCormick, an erstwhile army PTI and remedial gymnast, was already familiar to followers of local football. As manager of Wellingborough Town he was well known for his punishing pre-season schedules, based largely on stamina-sapping runs, repetitive lapping of the pitch and sprint work, all strictly monitored by pulse-rate recording. He regarded the assorted shapes and sizes lined up before him on the County Ground that morning with an element of sadistic pleasure. Many of the North East contingent had a serious fondness for beer and hearty portions and appeared poor athletic specimens. They absorbed Mac's opening words with a degree of trepidation.

'They're employing me for a week to get you fit or die in the attempt,' he proclaimed in a gravelly Scots accent. 'And you,' he went on, picking out the corpulent frame of Ollie Milburn for singular attention, 'will soon be rendered down.'

A bemused Ollie looked to David for clarification.

'He means he's going to get rid of your fat,' he explained. 'And he's got a lot to go at.'

On that first morning the players were dispatched on a two-mile run through the outskirts of Northampton. After a few hundred yards a breathless Milburn stopped for air on a bridge and promptly emptied his substantial breakfast into the stream below. Most eventually completed the course, but none as quickly as Brian Crump. When the remainder arrived back at the ground in dribs and drabs the all-rounder's achievement was lauded by their mentor. Little did he know that the resourceful Crump had unearthed a few coins from his pocket en-route and boarded a bus bound for Abington Avenue. After three days of Mac's routine, four players were injured and the rest increasingly disaffected. As David recalls, 'Far from getting us fit, he was putting us in hospital.' At last a deputation sought out Ken Turner with a clear warning: 'If he stays a few more days we'll have no team. We're cricketers, not bloody marathon runners.'

Mac left the next day.

For forty years, until his retirement in 1984, players' injuries were treated by the club physiotherapist, Jack Jennings. Genial Jack, a fixture at the County Ground, wintered with the town football club and moved seamlessly into a similar role with the cricketers during the summer. He was well-regarded enough to accompany the England football team to the Olympics in Melbourne and Rome, and later tour Australia with the MCC. Jack had worked at a rehabilitation centre for wounded servicemen in Bedford during the war and gave lead-swinging cricketers little sympathy. However, David remains sceptical of his therapeutic expertise.

'Jack was a qualified chiropodist and horse-racing aficionado who openly confessed that his treatment fell into two categories. "If it's a bruise, I give it a rub. If it's broken and the bone sticks through, I send them to hospital."'

Brian Crump was one of the most frequent occupants of Jack's treatment table. A renowned hypochondriac and racing enthusiast, the all-rounder was an avid consumer of vitamin pills purchased in vast quantities from Dr Barker, the Tunstall quack. Whether they actually helped him deliver his daily quota of thirty-five overs of penetrating seam is open to doubt but they certainly did little to prevent the aching limbs that sought regular relief from the physio's magic fingertips. On one occasion Brian was lying face-down on the slab receiving the benefit of an antiquated heat lamp suspended above his nether regions. Jack had spread his copy of *Sporting Life* over Brian's

backside and was engrossed in picking 'tanner doubles' from the list
of afternoon runners and riders and discussing form with the prostrate Crump, who was becoming increasingly agitated.

'Jack, the lamp's getting warm. Is it OK?'

The physio continued to study form, completely oblivious to
Crump's protestations.

'Jack, the bloody thing's red hot! Check it out will you!'

Again no response.

Suddenly the smouldering newspaper burst into flames and Brian
took flight, leaping from the table to avoid being burned alive.

Totally unrepentant, Jack later related the story to an amused
dressing room adding, 'When Crumpy shot off the table, he moved
quicker than he's ever done before. Injury cured!'

Interestingly, while many of his colleagues have suffered the familiar after effects of a body-punishing career in the field, Brian Crump
has required no surgery to those vastly over-worked joints. Testament, no doubt, to that smooth bowling action inherited from his
father Stanley and thoroughly honed in the 1,200 or so overs bowled
every season during his twelve-year stint with the club.

However, the less than rigorous approach to physical fitness and
the treatment of injuries was surpassed by the almost total lack of
concern for a player's mental wellbeing. The demands on professional
sportsmen to perform at a consistently high level or suffer the conse-
quences subjected them to inordinate pressure and some coped much
better than others. David's single-mindedness and resolve meant he
was rarely affected, relying on his considerable self-belief in technique
to outstay periods of lost form. Not everyone was as fortunate.

Two players in question, one a pace bowler and the other a spinner, suffered from a condition widely known amongst sportsmen as
the yips. Both were talented and experienced county cricketers and
masters of their art, but each suddenly and unaccountably lost the
ability to control their deliveries in match situations. David recalls
observing the opening bowler's tribulations from short-leg as he re-
peatedly sprayed the new ball all round the wicket.

'He was clearly a troubled man and had difficulty comprehending what was happening. I suggested he changed his grip to stop the ball from swinging away but it made no difference. He had a horrible game – and things didn't improve in the next few matches.'

Despite spending every available minute in the nets, where the player regained his usual control, as soon as he took to the field of play his unerring accuracy deserted him and he simply couldn't bowl straight. He was caught in a vicious cycle. The harder he tried the less effective he became and there was no one to turn to for advice beyond the close circle of teammates. While the players were getting changed before one game, a teammate went through to the shower room and happened upon an alarming sight. The troubled bowler was on his hands and knees staring at the seven pairs of boots lined up in a row before him, addressing them in plaintive tones.

'Which boots will bowl straight for me today?' he asked.

The observer slipped out of the room unnoticed and reported the scene to his fellow players who struggled to retain their composure, with sympathy doubtless in short supply.

Another sad case of a bowler losing his art was that of Fred Swarbrook, a very capable left-arm spinner who took 467 wickets at just under 30 apiece in his twelve year career in first-class cricket. In 1978 David enjoyed a most productive game for Northamptonshire against a Derbyshire side, which was beaten by an innings. He captured eleven wickets in the match and scored 130 runs; of the 100 overs delivered by the visitors' attack, the unfortunate Swarbrook managed just one, costing eleven runs.

'I'd heard he was having trouble,' he recalls, 'but he was just awful. He had absolutely no control of the ball, bowling a selection of over-pitched full tosses, long-hops and some which even bounced twice before reaching the bat. He was really quite dangerous because you could become over-confident facing such rubbish and get yourself out. Back in the pavilion he actually thanked me for not hitting him too far.'

The following year David left Northamptonshire and became captain of Derbyshire where he met up with Fred once more.

'I'd heard that he was seeing a psychiatrist in an attempt to curb his demons and asked him if the sessions were proving useful. He told me that he'd been advised to choose a pebble for luck, put it in his pocket, and rub it before delivering a ball. Remembering his problems the previous season I never bowled him and when I lost the captaincy a few games into the season took on the spinner's role myself.'

However, Swarbrook remained in the side batting in the lower order and wasn't called upon to bowl until a game against Lancashire at Aigburth in Liverpool in the middle of July. The match was memorable for several incidents, one of which was probably unique in the history of the game. Lancashire batted first and their openers Barry Wood and David Lloyd had scored 15 runs – including six no-balls and two wides – against some unaccountably erratic stuff from Bob Wincer and John Walters. As the players crossed over at the end of an over, umpire Dickie Bird turned to David and said, 'Steeley, something's wrong with this wicket.'

'Bad bowling, Dickie, that's what wrong.'

'No,' the official retorted. 'I'm pretty sure the wickets are not in line.'

Play was stopped, the groundsman summoned and the umpire's diagnosis proven. The wickets were out of alignment. A new game began.

Wood and Lloyd posted 103 second time around. By the middle of the afternoon Derbyshire had managed to remove the openers but were making few inroads into the middle order. The score eventually rose to 406 for four before Lancashire declared but, difficult though the bowlers' task had been, captain Peter Kirsten had refrained from using Swarbrook, perhaps to protect him from the mighty Clive Lloyd who hit 104 not out. The hosts' second innings followed the same pattern as the first when, with the total nearing 200 with just one wicket down, Kirsten announced that he was finally turning to the man with the pebble in his pocket.

'Why not?' he declared. 'It's a bloody circus anyway. Come and have a go, Fred. See if you can bowl it straight.'

The first over was a tidy maiden but then the yips began to take hold and he gradually lost his line and length.

'Don't worry,' his colleagues urged. 'Rub your pebble – or throw the ball away and bowl the pebble.'

In the final over of Fred's brief spell, Clive's namesake David, on his way to an undefeated 135, sent a ball soaring into the branches of one of the horse-chestnut trees that ringed the ground. Retrieving it from its resting place beneath the vast canopy, fielder Bob Wincer returned the ball with an accompanying rejoinder.

'Fancy taking conkers in July,' he shouted.

It proved to be Swarbrook's epitaph. It was his last Championship appearance for Derbyshire.

There is no doubt that the two bowlers would be better treated today. Support and advice may well have come from Jeremy Snape, the former Northamptonshire, Gloucestershire, Leicestershire and England cricketer and son of Keith, David's old friend and driving instructor from Brown Edge. Jeremy retrained as a sports psychologist after retiring from his playing career and now works with international sports teams and businesses on developing the winning mind-set, supporting the likes of Shane Warne and teams in the IPL, Big Bash, South Africa and Sri Lanka. He has interviewed many of the world's top performers to understand how they think under pressure:

All sport is best played instinctively and everyone who has experienced what it feels like to bowl a great ball, play a great shot or take a great catch will know that in that moment there was very little 'thinking' going on. The problem comes when we start to worry too much about what happens if we fail. This takes our mind away from the tactics and skills needed to win the next ball and creates an inner battle against ourselves where all we can think about is failure, shame and what people will think of us afterwards. As this fear grips, we start to focus too much on all the micromovements needed to deliver the perfect ball and we become obsessed with mechanics.

Bowling is a high specialised biomechanical skill when you break it down. Bowlers run through the crease in a fraction of a second, turning

*David shares a glass with
Jeremy Snape.*

their hips, twisting their torso, rotating their legs and whipping through both arms and effecting the perfect release point. When bowlers are bowling well they are thinking what they want to do to the batsman, they hold the power and they are thinking about their competitive intent towards the batsman rather than their left elbow being in a certain angle as it brushes past their ribs. When bowlers think about this tiny component of bowling in isolation, it stops the essential natural flow and highlights each mechanical element in a jerky sequence.

Players are constantly assessing the strategy, risks and rewards of each delivery choice and technical tweak but when this volume becomes negative in the head then it can create problems. When poor deliveries get smashed, shame and self-doubt can spiral to the point where people experience panic attacks, scrambled thinking and even a heavy sensation in their body which makes them feel like they are bowling cannon balls in slow motion.

The modern era seems to have even more analysis, media opinion and judgement than ever at a time when the rewards from the top game are life changing. It's so important for players to develop the mental skills they need to be resilient and aware of how to control these negative thinking spirals.

Having worked with and interviewed some of the world's top performers through my work at Sporting Edge, it's interesting to hear their strategies. Shane Warne for example remembers these feelings of tension rising in the World Cup semi-final and he took longer in his run up, controlled his breathing and asked himself 'how do I get this guy out?' that is a very different mindset to the rushed mechanical thinking of the panic mode. Another Australian legend Glenn McGrath said that if he was bowling the last ball of a world cup final, he'd plan his delivery make a full commitment to it and then sing a song in his run up. While this may seem difficult to believe, it's a great antidote to over thinking. By thinking about your breathing patterns or singing a song, the world's best performers are switching off their conscious brain which allows their instinct to take over.

The lesson highlights how the outcome is out of our control but the process of delivering your best ball is very much in your control, we need to focus on our inputs rather than letting our fears of a bad outcome affect how we approach the delivery in the first place. When we set a clear committed strategy and a trust our skills and muscle memory to deliver our best ball then we've got a great chance of success. There is no doubt though that before we can win the next ball against the batsman, we need to win the battle in our own mind.

17

CLOSE OF PLAY

David bowled a lot of overs on his return to Northamptonshire from Derbyshire in 1982. In one match, the fixture against Gloucestershire at Bristol that July, he delivered a total of seventy-two overs, taking four wickets in the first innings and five in the second. In addition, his 74 first-innings runs helped secure a nine-wicket win. Coincidentally, it was a game at Bristol two years later that contributed to David's decision to bring his first-class career to an end. The cumulative effect of twenty years on the county circuit was contributing to worsening pain in the hip region, caused by severe arthritis in the joint. Stiff and literally unable to move after another long bowling stint and two lengthy spells at the wicket he decided to seek out a meeting with secretary Ken Turner to discuss his future in the game. Turner was an inpatient in Northampton General Hospital at the time and an intimate chat took place at his bedside. The conversation reflected their mutual respect, fostered over a long association at Wantage Road, and The Sec was typically forthright in offering advice.

'The contract's there if you want it,' he said. 'But don't pick it up. Don't spoil it now after the career you've had.'

The words hit home and the final fixture of the season at Worcester proved to be David's last match in the County Championship.

The occasion did not pass without ceremony. For much of his playing career David favoured a pair of long, flannelette underpants nicknamed the Burma Co-ops by teammates for their similarity to the voluminous khaki shorts worn by soldiers during the wartime campaign in the Far East. Think *It Ain't Half Hot, Mum*. The pants had featured in an incident during the 1982 season when the county played Kent at Folkestone. Umpire Nigel Plews' loud no-ball call against David was greeted by widespread applause from the Northamptonshire players.

'What's going on?' he asked the bowler.

'They're clapping my hundredth no-ball of the season,' David replied, 'and you've had a hell of a lot to do with it. Look up there!'

He pointed to the flagpole alongside the pavilion from which a familiar item from his cricketing wardrobe fluttered in the stiff breeze.

'They're my Burma Co-op drawers. That's Lamby's work. Still, they'll be nice and aired when they come down!'

And so, at the close of the final day's play at Worcester, prankster-in-chief Allan Lamb gathered the players together on the steps of the famous pavilion to conduct the ritual burning of the Burmas, bringing the curtain down on David's illustrious career.

In an article in *Wisden Cricket Monthly* from March 1985 entitled 'The grey-haired gent who saved England,' John Arlott recorded a 'fond memoir to the departed David Steele,' in which he savours the achievements of a 'deliberately unspectacular, dedicated careful man, rarely known to shout.' There is an affectionate and appreciative account of his brief Test career against Australia and the West Indies with the focus on that time, ten years earlier, when he became, 'as splendidly as unexpectedly, a national hero. Not simply a cricketing hero but one who rose above the limits of sporting interest to reach the hearts of the British people in quite epic fashion. Certainly he stood higher in national esteem than any post-war English cricketer except perhaps – in a different fashion – Denis Compton in 1947-48.'

It was back to the printing industry, but the flannels were not packed away for good. News of his retirement had reached the sec-

After cricket, David continued a successful career in the printing industry.

retary of West Bromwich Dartmouth Cricket Club, members of the Birmingham League, who offered him the professional's role for the 1985 season at a generous salary which, he recalls, financed the Aga still gracing the kitchen of his Geddington home. The highly competitive league produced excellent fixtures including games against Warwickshire seconds, led by Alan Oakman, the former Sussex player who fielded at short-leg during the celebrated Laker Test match at Old Trafford in 1956. David skippered the team, bowling unchanged from one end while rotating at the other, and almost led them to the title which was eventually decided in a play-off against rivals Moseley in the last game of the campaign. Chasing a modest total, West Brom reached 70 for none before the failing light, and Moseley's South African fast bowler, Brian McMillan, contributed to a batting collapse and eventual defeat.

David also renewed his acquaintance with the Minor Counties Championship during the season, appearing for Bedfordshire along with cricketing friends John Wake and Andy Pearson. This led to what his many admirers hoped would be a final glorious tussle with a West Indian fast bowler of more recent vintage. Courtney Walsh was a member of Gloucestershire's outstanding attack along with the likes of David 'Syd' Lawrence, Kevin Curran and David Graveney in their NatWest Trophy tie against Bedfordshire at Wardown Park, Luton, in July 1985. David, pushing 44, sent down a dozen tidy overs for 29 as the part-timers restricted their visitors to 268 for six. He then strode out to open the Bedfordshire innings with Kevin Gentle against Lawrence and Walsh. Another stirring display of plucky batsmanship against the odds? The romantics in the crowd – not to mention a few in the press box – were disappointed. Walsh cleaned David up for a duck and Gentle, offered the dubious privilege by his illustrious partner of facing the first ball 'as it's a special occasion', took a crack on the head for his trouble. Wake, later Oundle School's long-serving master-in-charge of cricket, top-scored with 37 as Gloucestershire closed the match out with ease.

During his benefit year in 1975, which fortuitously coincided with his spectacular introduction to Test cricket, David had toured Northamptonshire meeting groups up and down the county raising money for his appeal which eventually raised £25,500, easily a club record at the time. It often involved making a brief speech, a task performed with some reluctance. At a rather more prestigious event, held in his honour at the Savoy Hotel later that year, David was invited to offer a vote of thanks to the main speaker, the respected cricketing journalist Crawford White. He stood up, mumbled 'thank you' and then, to his acute embarrassment, couldn't remember the speaker's name. Graciously, Crawford came to his rescue, with a kindly intervention.

'If he'd batted like he's spoken we wouldn't be here today!'

From that moment David resolved to be always 'spot on' when addressing gatherings publically. Taking advice and learning from accomplished veterans of the circuit, such as the urbane and witty Chairman of the Northamptonshire County League, Harry Johnson, he began to carve out another career as a popular after-dinner speaker, visiting cricket societies around the British Isles. One such event was held at the RAC Club in London's Piccadilly in May 2005. Hosted by the MCC's John Fingleton, his fellow speaker was Frances Edmonds, wife of Phil, the former Middlesex and England spinner. During the meal Phil turned to David and said, 'Those three balls I bowled you at Wellingborough School didn't do you any good, did they?'

David was nonplussed. 'What do you mean?' he asked.

His thoughts returned to the fixture at the school ground during the 1977 season. The scorecard starkly states, 'Steele bowled Edmonds 1'. But David's recollection of his brief innings is of the difficulty he had that afternoon in picking up the flight of the ball against the dark background of the trees above the sightscreen behind the bowler's arm. He'd missed three balls in succession – something he'd never done before.

Phil Edmonds continued. 'Alec Bedser, the Chairman of the England selectors, was there to witness your innings that afternoon which, he maintained, confirmed his opinion that you couldn't play spin.'

Speaking at the RAC Club, the occasion during which David discovered the 'reason' he was dropped by the England selectors.

The explanation still rankles years later. David's hurt at missing out on the series in India or of possibly resurrecting his Test career in Pakistan the following winter remains palpable. He was not alone in feeling aggrieved. In the aforementioned article, John Arlott reflects on David's omission from the touring party: 'I thought that it was, to say the least, gross ingratitude in view of all he had done for English cricket. Surely he deserved his place. But as the EW Swanton of the Elizabethan Age puts it: 'Blow, blow thou winter wind/ Thou art not so unkind/ As man's ingratitude'

In 1976 David had acquired a run-down house with extensive grounds on the edge of the historic village of Geddington. He spent over two years renovating the property before finally taking up residence in April 1979. As he recalls, 'Ron Ashby, a colleague and van driver at Staples Press, delivered the furniture on the day I set off for a new career at Derbyshire.'

He soon settled into village life, his children Arran and Mark attended the local school, and friendships were forged with members of the community. It wasn't long after severing his connections with top-flight cricket that he was approached by Olly Dalziel, a local plumber, with a view to David dusting off his flannels and turning out for Weekley and Warkton in Division One of the Northamptonshire County League. Despite its primitive facilities and unpredictable batting strip, the picturesque ground at Boughton Park on the Duke of Buccleuch's estate provided David with a productive extension to his lengthy playing career.

There were occasional reminders of his glorious past, such as a game against an Isham side including John 'Doc' Dye, his former Northamptonshire teammate. 'The Doc was one of the best I played with and, like me, he still retained that competitive edge. I was at the non-striker's end when he bowled one ball to Fred Beasley, no mean batsman at that level, which pitched on leg and flew past the off-stump. I shouted "You were lucky to miss that one, Fred," but I wasn't so fortunate when he did me a few balls later. We only managed 140 and they made a good start chasing the score down. Dye was walking round the boundary looking too pleased with himself but when the wickets started to tumble and panic stations set in I let him have it. "I want to see you with your pads on!" I hollered across the outfield, and got my wish when he came out to bat at number eleven with four runs wanted off the last over to win the match. His partner came charging down the wicket to me but swung and missed offering a simple stumping to our keeper, who unaccountably "lost" the ball and with it the stumping opportunity. On retrieving it he threw it to the bowler's end where I kicked it away in disgust. The match was lost and the Doc had the last laugh.'

David has happy recollections of his three-year association with the club and of the numerous characters that brightened his twilight days. His fellow opener Ron Kershaw, who once played with Everton Weekes at Bacup in the Lancashire League; Terry Walklate, a prolific batsman and slow bowler, whose weakness for regularly slipping a

A suitable ending with Weekley and Warkton, 1989.
Back: Colin Issitt, Paul Burrows, Frank Watts, Clive Hawkins, Ron Kershaw, Dave Walklate. Front: Andy Tilley, Karl Peasnall, Chris Payne, Richard Marshall, Fred Beasley, David Steele.

leg spin delivery into every over of off-spin gifted the batsman a certain boundary, was much to David's frustration; the dedicated and dependable Karl Peasnall; Colin Issitt, who had two slips and a gully while bowling everything down the leg side. And an image of Dalziel, lying flat on his back after taking a catch on the boundary at Stony Stratford, is etched in David's memory as clearly as any from his days in county cricket.

He enjoyed the company and, not unexpectedly, enjoyed success with both bat and ball. In 1988, the second of his three seasons, he topped the division's bowling averages with thirty-six wickets at 8.76 and bowed out the following year by finishing second in the batting list scoring 337 runs at an average of 42.12. No wonder the league yearbook notes that he 'retired before the 1990 season and was missed by the side'. David remains a supporter of the club and, in the summer of 2017, opened the new pavilion on a ground much re-modelled since his playing days there.

There was a time when county cricketers worked a six-day week. Three-day Championship matches were played on a Wednesday, Thursday and Friday with the new game beginning on Saturday and continuing on Monday and Tuesday. David often took advantage of his day of rest to take Carol and her mother to nearby Stamford for lunch. Its architectural delights are extolled in Alec Clifton Taylor's renowned *Six English Towns* but David's appreciation extended to a grade-two listed building known as the Lady Anne's Hotel, where he regularly enjoyed its famous Sunday lunches.

For some years the hotelier, Geoff Hastings, had entertained and accommodated clients from Benson and Hedges who, knowing of his passion for sport and particularly cricket, often invited him as guest of honour at prestigious sporting events. One such occasion was a rugby league cup final at Wembley when two coachloads of supporters from Yorkshire called at the hotel en-route to the stadium for a full English breakfast and to collect their packed lunches. Then, returning from the game, the coaches called back to the Lady Anne's in order for the fans to enjoy its celebrated roast beef dinner.

Geoff reciprocated by hosting a cricket match on August bank holiday Monday between his eleven and a team of Yorkshire League players representing Benson and Hedges at nearby Burghley Park in aid of the Macmillan cancer charity. The Benson and Hedges side, named the Bent Edges, thrashed Geoff's team and at the end of the game he told them 'to bring a decent team next year'.

The match became a fixture on the cricketing calendar and, some years later, when lunching at the hotel after one of the games, David expressed his disappointment at not being involved.

'Why didn't you give me a call?' he asked. 'I want to play next year.'

Geoff was delighted. 'Would you like to bring a team?' he replied.

David's answer was unequivocal.

'I've tasted the beef, and you're on. I've never played at Burghley Park.'

It was the beginning of a long and successful association which saw David's teams, comprising such eminent players as Mushtaq Mohammad, John Dye, Brian Crump, (who never missed), Sarfraz Nawaz, Bob Taylor, Geoff Miller, Alan Hodgson and Peter Willey, compete against sides from Nottinghamshire and Yorkshire. Both Fred Trueman and Garfield Sobers had stints as non-playing captains of the Bent Edges, whose sides included notable Test and county stars like Basharat Hassan and, on one memorable occasion, Chris Broad.

Broad's appearance coincided with that of the former Middlesex and Northamptonshire player, the Honourable Tim Lamb, who was then chief executive of the Test and County Cricket Board. David still chuckles at Mike Brearley's observation when, on learning that Lamb was about to move to Wantage Road, he questioned the Middlesex captain on Lamb's merits as a medium-pacer.

'He needs a lot of bowling,' Brearley remarked, 'but you can't afford to give it to him.'

Before the start of the match at Burghley House, Lamb approached the captains clutching a bag of white cricket balls. 'Can we use these balls today?' he asked. 'Forty-five overs to test them out.'

Unfortunately for Lamb, the innovation proved an unlucky one when he was dismissed in a bizarre and unfortunate manner. Chris Broad bowled the first five balls of his over with his left hand before switching to his right (without notifying the batsman or umpire) for the final delivery, which struck the batsman on the pads. The Bent Edge players appealed and umpire David Lowe raised his finger – incorrectly. Poor Lamb walked but, aware of the laws, chuntered that he was not out all the way back to the pavilion.

A particular highlight was the occasion when one of David's old adversaries registered his considerable presence. Visitors to Stamford would have been surprised to see signs at the roadside en-route to Burghley bearing the words: 'Dennis Lillee is here today.'

Players taking part in the fixture were accommodated at the Lady Anne's on the Sunday night preceding the match and following the traditional roast beef dinner were required to stand up and do a turn. Over the years the hotel became a focal point for cricketing enthusiasts, its bar decorated with memorabilia donated by the many celebrities that graced its environs. Charity events, such as sports-

Good times at the Lady Anne's with Mushtaq Mohammad, Frank Tyson, Fred Trueman, Roy Virgin and Frank Hayes.

men's dinners, were immensely popular. Fred Trueman and David were regulars but others, including Geoff Miller, Richard Hadlee, Jeff Thomson, Ian Botham, Frank Tyson and Brian Close featured on the impressive list of speakers. Geoff Hastings' wife, Anne, a Yorkshire girl and vital partner in the hotel's success, had never attended a cricket dinner but made an exception for Close. Unfortunately, a group known as the Motley Crew plied Brian with drinks prior to his speech. When he finally stood up, considerably the worse for wear, his delivery quickly degenerated as the alcohol took effect and muddling his cue cards he began to repeat his stories. Much amused, his audience were happy to forgive the great man, unlike Anne who left the table furious at her hero's humiliation.

Geoff Hastings' friendship with Trueman led to the formation of the Fred Trueman Cricket League in 2007. The first venture, a dinner addressed by the great bowler himself, raised £4,000 and subsequent events, boosted by National Lottery grants, enabled teams from secondary schools in the Lincolnshire area to participate in a 20-over competition, each equipped with £500 worth of playing kit and whites. Support for the project came from variety of sources. One day Geoff received a phone call from South Africa. It was Geoffrey Boycott apologising that he couldn't attend one of Fred's talks but would 'do a dinner free for the Fred Trueman schools charity' when he was back in England as it was for 'a good cause which I'd very much like to support'.

Geoff Hastings retired from the hotel business some years ago but retains his involvement in the game he loves. The Trueman League has expanded from its original base and continues to flourish while its co-founder is actively involved in the Border Counties Youth Cricket Association and has recently joined the Trustees at the Cricket Society Trust, which supports disabled cricketers.

From an early age David was an avid reader of the sports pages in the *Sentinel*, his local newspaper. There he followed the fortunes of the fabled footballer, Uncle Freddie Steele, and his cricketing counterpart, Uncle Stanley Crump. His own achievements were recognised in 1975 when he became the first winner of the Stoke-on-Trent

Sports Personality of the Year. In 2011 he and squash world champion Angela Smith were inducted into the City of Stoke Sporting Hall of Fame, joining such celebrated inductees as footballers Sir Stanley Matthews, Gordon Banks, Denis Smith, Dennis Wilshaw, Roy Sproson, darts star Phil Taylor, Olympic hockey champion Imran Sherwani and cycling great Les West. The occasion, at the city's King's Hall, was attended by 350 including guest of honour, former athlete David Moorcroft.

David's family, wife Carol, children Arran and Mark and their wives, and Brian and Lyn Crump were also present, seated at a table adorned with a cardboard cut-out of Freddie Steele. They all enjoyed a most convivial evening, the ladies being particularly impressed by the presence of the cricket-loving father of another successful son of Stoke, singer Robbie Williams.

Such formal recognition is always appreciated but, despite his exploits with bat and ball being consigned to the yellowing pages of *Wisden*, David is occasionally accosted by strangers keen to talk about his days at the crease. One such occasion occurred in 2014. After suffering extreme pain in his knee David was recommended to see Stephen Godsiff, an orthopaedic consultant at Leicester General Hospital. The offending joint was x-rayed and the pair met to discuss the findings. David retains a vivid recollection of that first appointment.

> Mr Godsiff came into the room holding the x-ray films, gave them a superficial glance and then threw them into the corner. 'Very nice to see you,' he said. 'I love cricket and often watched you play.' He then proceeded to run through my career picking out matches and recalling details with unerring accuracy. It was flattering but I was more concerned about the condition of my knee.
>
> 'What about the x-rays?' I asked. He was fairly dismissive.
>
> 'We'll have another look in about three months,' he said.

Mr Godsiff didn't appear at the next appointment and his place was taken by an Indian doctor whose turban reminded David of the peerless Bedi, and another six months passed before they were reunited. Once again the subject of cricket dominated and, in the course of conversation, David recounted Sir Len Hutton's description of his batting technique in which he always referred to his top hand as 'life' and his bottom hand as 'death'.

The tale assumed significance during David's operation which took place some weeks later. He had opted for an epidural injection which meant that he was conscious during the procedure, a big sheet separating his upper body from his legs where the action was taking place. The consultant, dressed rather like a bee-keeper, was hammering away at David's knee with a mallet, blood and bone spurting up on the sheet.

'Can I talk to the surgeon?' the patient asked, anxious as to the progress of the operation. He received a nod in reply.

'Stephen,' he said. 'Is it life or is it death?'

The cricket-mad consultant grinned behind his mask, waved the implement in his left hand, proclaimed, 'It's life!' and continued the assault.

David made a complete recovery.

As with so many momentous sporting occasions, enthusiasts, and particularly those of a certain age, can recall exactly where they were on the day a thirty-three-year-old cricketer plucked from comparative obscurity at unfashionable Northamptonshire came to England's rescue. The eulogies have been recorded for posterity, scorecards do not lie, the legacy is assured. But the qualities displayed on that memorable morning at Lord's were at the core of his character. The striving to be the best he could possibly be, illustrated so vividly in those thrice weekly net practices under the demanding tutelage of Stanley Crump, is reflected in so many aspects of this ordinary man's extraordinary life. As a professional cricketer, print salesman, husband, father and grandfather he brought the full force of his personality to his every action.

Steele by name, steel by nature.

POSTSCRIPT

Sentimentality isn't a character trait you associate immediately with Northamptonshire County Cricket Club. For most of its history it hasn't been able to afford it. Particularly during the Ken Turner era, hard-headed decision-making was the norm – even if it meant dispensing with the services of devoted stalwarts like Brian Reynolds and, as we've seen, Brian Crump. As far back as 1921, the Honorary Secretary of twenty-three years, AJ 'Pat' Darnell, complained bitterly about 'ingratitude' after being ousted (along with other members of the old guard) in a polite but ruthless coup.

But in April 2018, following a decade and a half of gentle lobbying, the club launched a Hall of Fame as a tangible and permanent way of honouring individuals who have given outstanding service on or off the field. The co-authors of Northamptonshire's official history (one of whom is co-author of this book) took on the task of selecting the first twelve inductees, the idea being that supporters would then make nominations for a further three choices to be announced at the end of the season.

A special breakfast for sponsors and board members at Wantage Road was the occasion chosen to unveil the distinguished dozen. As the county team practised outside, ready to tackle Warwickshire in the first home Championship match of the campaign, a short video with photographs and information about the Hall's inaugural members was shown on the big screen.

George Thompson was first up, the man who batted and bowled Northamptonshire into first-class cricket, together with his long-time brother-in-arms Billy East. Mean and moody left-arm paceman Edward 'Nobby' Clark and brilliant batsman Fred Bakewell, both stars of the tough inter-war years. The loyal and elegant Dennis Brookes. John Bull incarnate, Freddie Brown. Frank Tyson – the 'typhoon' who blew away the Aussies in 1954-55 – and peerless wicketkeeper (and idiosyncratic skipper) Keith Andrew. Colin Milburn, buccaneering hitter whose career ended, like Bakewell's, in a tragic car crash. Then a gentle ripple of laughter went around the room as a familiar face popped up under the label 'the bank clerk goes to war'.

David was present for the announcement; one of only three living inductees, along with Bishan Bedi and Allan Lamb. He told anyone within earshot that he was honoured, 'but Mushie should have been there.' Doubtless he will be before long.

None of David's fellow first-footers prompted the same degree of recognition and affection that morning. Even forty-three years after his season in the sun, those Northamptonshire supporters of a certain age remembered – and smiled.

Enjoying a happy retirement with Carol.

THE CLUB IS GRATEFUL TO BACAL CONSTRUCTION LTD. FOR SPC

This card does not necessarily include the fall of the last wicket

AUG 5th, 7th and 8th, 1972   N O R T H A M P T O N S H I R E

	Northamptonshire	1st Innings		2nd Innings	
1	A Tait	b Massie	0		
2	G Cook	st Taber b Gleeson	62	c Chappell b Gleeson	24
3	D S Steele	lbw Massie	19	not out	60
4	M Mohammed	not out	88	c Marsh b Lillee	30
5	†P J Watts	lbw Gleeson	0	not out	3
6	B S Crump	lbw Watson	3	run out	1
7	P Willey	lbw Watson	8		
8	R M H Cottam	st Marsh b Gleeson	0		
9	‡L A Johnson	b Watson	0		
10	B S Bedi	b Watson	4		
11	J C J Dye	b Watson	4		
		Extras	22	Extras	7
			210		125

†Captain
‡Wicketkeeper

1st Ins. 1-1   2-53   3-142   4-142   5-149   6-171   7-178   8-191   9-195   10-210
2nd Ins. 1-38   2-103   3-104   4-   5-   6-   7-   8-   9-   10-

Bowling Analysis	O	M	R	Wk	N	W	O	M	R	Wk	N	W
Massie	24	10	50	2	4	1						
Lillee	12	2	35	0	6	....	7	0	25	1	1	....
Colley	9	2	29	0	2	—	6.5	2	27	0	3	....
Watson	14	3	36	5	1	—	4	0	11	0		—
Gleeson	11	1	38	3	6	—	9	4	26	1	2	—
Inverarity							6	0	39	0	....	—

Umpires— W E Phillipson and J Arnold

Hours of play—1st Day, 11.30-6.30   2nd Day, 11.30-6.30

A NEW BALL may be

1st Innings points, awarded in the first 85 overs of each innings

The Northamptonshire innings against the touring Australians in 1972 – a historic victory for the home county.

Statistics

Test matches

Year	Venue	Runs	Balls	6s	4s	Bowling	Ct
1975	Lord's	50	103	-	9	0.4-0-1-1	-
v Aus		45	111	-	6	9-4-19-1	-
1975	Headingley	73	169	-	8	-	1
v Aus		92	222	1	7	0	1
1975	The Oval	39	80	1	5	2-1-1-0	2
v Aus		66	175	-	6	-	-
1976	Trent Bge	106	296	-	9	-	1
v WI		6	20	-	1	-	-
1976	Lord's	7	20	-	1	-	-
v WI		64	206	-	7	-	-
1976	Old Traff	20	23	-	3	-	1
v WI		15	27	1	1	-	-
1976	Headingley	4	13	-	-	-	1
v WI		0	2	-	-	-	-
1976	The Oval	44	88	-	6	3-0-18-0	-
v WI		42	145	-	5	-	-

First-class matches
Batting and fielding

Year	M	Inn	NO	Runs	HS	Avg	100s	50s	Ct
1963	8	12	2	116	27	11.60	-	-	12
1964	19	31	5	773	74	29.73	-	5	20
1965	30	47	4	1193	104	27.74	1	5	40
1966	30	48	6	1170	118*	27.85	2	3	33
1967	32	47	5	1095	93	26.07	-	6	40
1968	27	44	4	827	80	20.67	-	4	25
1969	14	19	7	445	101*	37.08	1	1	14
1970	22	39	3	913	90*	25.36	-	6	26
1971	26	48	3	1577	140*	35.04	3	8	32
1972	22	39	8	1618	131	52.19	5	7	25
1973	24	40	6	1402	129*	41.23	3	8	27
1974	21	36	3	1022	104	30.96	1	7	20
1975	21	39	3	1756	126*	48.77	3	11	26
75-6	4	7	2	356	110*	71.20	1	2	5
1976	18	34	4	992	139	33.06	2	6	17
1977	19	33	4	938	117*	32.34	2	3	21
1978	21	36	5	1182	130	38.12	3	9	24
1979	23	38	8	1190	127*	39.66	2	7	22
1980	20	31	7	698	86*	29.08	-	3	19
80-1	3	6	-	120	52	20.00	-	1	6
1981	21	32	3	902	137	31.10	1	5	15
1982	25	36	13	853	74*	37.08	-	4	19
1983	25	31	6	569	60	22.76	-	3	29
1984	25	39	13	639	78*	24.57	-	3	29
TOT	**500**	**812**	**124**	**22346**	**140***	**32.47**	**30**	**117**	**546**

First-class matches
Centuries (30)

Score	For	Opponents	Venue	Year
104	Northants	Essex	Northampton	1965
118*	Northants	Leicestershire	Leicester	1966
117	Northants	Gloucestershire	Bristol	1966
101*	Northants	Oxford Uni	Northampton	1969
118	Northants	Lancashire	Northampton	1971
140*	Northants	Worcestershire	Worcester	1971
107*	Northants	Leicestershire	Leicester	1971
122	Northants	Oxford Uni	Oxford	1972
107*	Northants	Warwickshire	Birmingham	1972
131	Northants	Surrey	Northampton	1972
109*	Northants	Leicestershire	Leicester	1972
106*	Northants	Kent	Dover	1972
129*	Northants	Kent	Northampton	1973
105	Northants	Worcestershire	Kidderminster	1973
116	Northants	Leicestershire	Northampton	1973
104	Northants	Kent	Folkestone	1974
126*	Northants	Glamorgan	Northampton	1975
102	Northants	Worcestershire	Worcester	1975
102	Northants	Australians	Northampton	1975
110*	DH Robins' XI	Western Province	Cape Town	1975-6
139	Northants	Middlesex	Lord's	1976
106	England	West Indies	Nottingham	1976
106	Northants	Warwickshire	Northampton	1977
117*	Northants	Surrey	The Oval	1977
117	Northants	Worcestershire	Northampton	1978
102*	Northants	Yorkshire	Harrogate	1978
130	Northants	Derbyshire	Northampton	1978
122*	Derbyshire	Warwickshire	Chesterfield	1979
127*	Derbyshire	Indians	Derby	1979
137	Derbyshire	Somerset	Taunton	1981

First-class matches
Bowling

Year	Balls	Runs	Wkts	Avg	Best	5wI	10wM
1963	600	338	12	28.16	4-101	-	-
1964	1426	538	27	19.92	4-15	-	-
1965	1734	672	28	24.00	6-40	1	-
1966	1410	505	29	17.41	8-29	1	-
1967	1803	693	26	26.61	4-30	-	-
1968	807	332	13	25.53	3-30	-	-
1969	618	297	8	37.12	2-42	-	-
1970	364	139	8	17.37	3-17	-	-
1971	1823	813	40	20.32	6-52	1	-
1972	229	93	5	18.60	4-12	-	-
1973	475	146	7	20.85	4-28	-	-
1974	966	405	13	31.15	3-68	-	-
1975	453	148	11	13.45	4-37	-	-
75-6	153	54	5	10.80	3-20	-	-
1976	185	111	2	55.50	1-0	-	-
1977	176	68	1	68.00	1-0	-	-
1978	2271	976	37	26.37	6-36	3	1
1979	3022	1459	48	30.39	6-91	2	-
1980	2580	1221	54	22.61	7-133	4	1
80-1	180	79	4	19.75	3-29	-	-
1981	2418	1019	46	22.15	7-53	4	-
1982	4530	1846	70	26.37	6-59	6	1
1983	4068	1460	68	21.47	5-48	2	-
1984	4392	2100	61	34.42	5-86	2	-
TOT	**36693**	**15511**	**623**	**24.89**	**8-29**	**26**	**3**

First-class matches
Five or more wickets in an innings (26)

Figures	For	Opponents	Venue	Year
6-40	Northants	Derbyshire	Northampton	1965
8-29	Northants	Lancashire	Northampton	1966
6-52	Northants	Oxford Uni	Oxford	1971
6-36	Northants	Derbys (1st inn)	Northampton	1978
5-39	Northants	Derbys (2nd inn)	Northampton	1978
5-58	Northants	Hampshire	Northampton	1978
5-40	Derbyshire	Lancashire	Chesterfield	1979
6-91	Derbyshire	Hampshire	Basingstoke	1979
5-52	Derbyshire	Hampshire	Chesterfield	1980
5-74	Derbyshire	Glamorgan	Derby	1980
5-45	Derbyshire	Kent	Dartford	1980
7-133	Derbyshire	Nottinghamshire	Worksop	1980
6-77	Derbyshire	Warwickshire	Derby	1981
7-53	Derbyshire	Kent	Derby	1981
7-85	Derbyshire	Leicestershire	Derby	1981
5-62	Derbyshire	Glamorgan	Swansea	1981
5-71	Northants	Gloucestershire	Bristol	1982
5-32	Northants	Sussex	Eastbourne	1982
6-59	Northants	Hampshire	Northampton	1982
5-50	Northants	Leicestershire	Northampton	1982
5-105	Northants	Essex (1st inn)	Chelmsford	1982
5-44	Northants	Essex (2nd inn)	Chelmsford	1982
5-48	Northants	Yorkshire	Bradford	1983
5-67	Northants	Yorkshire	Northampton	1983
5-86	Northants	Lancashire	Southport	1984
5-122	Northants	Nottinghamshire	Nottingham	1984

The 5-74 against Glamorgan in 1980 included a hat-trick.

First-class matches
Catches

David Steele held 546 catches in first-class cricket. The bowlers off whom he took most catches are shown below:

48: DS Steele (caught and bowled)
47: H Sully
45: BS Crump
33: BS Bedi
26: BJ Griffiths
24: P Willey
23: Mushtaq Mohammad
20: Sarfraz Nawaz, A Hodgson
19: JCJ Dye
17: RMH Cottam, PJ Watts
16: JDF Larter
13: MK Kettle, ME Scott, JW Swinburne
11: CJ Tunnicliffe
10: RR Bailey, NA Mallender

List A matches
Batting and fielding

Year	M	Inn	NO	Runs	HS	Avg	100s	50s	Ct
1965	2	2	-	21	14	10.50	-	-	2
1966	1	1	-	8	8	8.00	-	-	-
1967	3	3	-	102	54	34.00	-	1	3
1968	3	2	-	55	34	27.50	-	-	3
1969	6	6	-	35	27	5.83	-	-	1
1970	12	10	1	139	58	15.44	-	1	6
1971	17	16	2	316	71*	22.57	-	1	5
1972	19	19	2	442	56	26.00	-	2	8
1973	19	17	1	320	60	20.00	-	2	3
1974	18	18	3	345	76	23.00	-	2	9
1975	20	20	2	536	109	29.77	1	1	5
75-6	1	1	-	19	19	19.00	-	-	-
1976	16	14	3	254	57	23.09	-	1	1
1977	20	16	3	390	64	30.00	-	4	7
1978	14	11	3	161	52	20.12	-	1	4
1979	21	17	2	304	81*	20.26	-	2	7
1980	20	18	2	443	71	27.68	-	1	10
1981	22	16	2	290	89*	20.71	-	1	9
1982	11	8	3	107	28	21.40	-	-	2
1983	4	3	2	59	38	59.00	-	-	1
1984	10	5	3	35	14	17.50	-		4
1985	1	1	-	0	0	0.00	-	-	1
TOT	**260**	**224**	**34**	**4381**	**109**	**23.05**	**1**	**20**	**91**

David Steele's only century in List A cricket was 109 for Northamptonshire against Cambridgeshire at March in 1975 (Gillette Cup 1st round).

He won the Man of the Match award for Derbyshire against Suffolk at Bury St Edmunds in 1981 (NatWest Trophy 1st round).

List A matches
Bowling

Year	Balls	Runs	Wkts	Avg	Best	Econ	4w
1965	24	16	0	-	-	4.00	-
1966	6	4	0	-	-	4.00	-
1967	-	-	-	-	-	-	-
1968	36	48	0	-	-	8.00	-
1969	114	88	1	88.00	1-43	4.63	-
1970	-	-	-	-	-	-	-
1971	48	46	0	-	-	5.75	-
1972	118	96	3	32.00	2-54	4.88	-
1973	90	68	1	68.00	1-20	4.53	-
1974	268	216	4	54.00	2-32	4.83	-
1975	90	82	0	-	-	5.46	-
75-6	-	-	-	-	-	-	-
1976	6	9	0	-	-	9.00	-
1977	48	32	2	16.00	2-23	4.00	-
1978	48	37	1	37.00	1-37	4.62	-
1979	594	332	18	18.44	4-21	3.35	1
1980	372	229	10	22.90	3-10	3.69	-
1981	409	302	13	23.23	3-36	4.43	-
1982	410	252	12	21.00	3-27	3.69	-
1983	168	99	6	16.50	3-23	3.19	-
1984	384	305	10	30.50	4-35	4.76	1
1985	72	29	0	-	-	2.41	-
TOT	**3323**	**2290**	**81**	**28.27**	**4-21**	**4.13**	**2**

David Steele's best bowling in List A cricket was 4-21 for Derbyshire against Nottinghamshire at Derby in 1979 in the John Player League.

ACKNOWLEDGEMENTS

The Steele family: for their infectious enthusiasm for the project; Carol, for sandwiches, coffee, cake and moral support; Arran and Mark, for their insightful contributions about growing up with Dad; brother John; and cousin Brian Crump.

The cricketing family: Geoffrey Boycott, for his inimitable foreword: Mushtaq Mohammad, Rob Bailey, Geoff Cook, Jim Watts, Roy Virgin and Dennis Lillee for their personal recollections.

Frank Hayes, for his colourful memories of working with David at Oakham School.

Stuart Broad, for the generous testimony to David's influence on his cricketing career.

Jeremy Snape, for his professional analysis.

Geoff Hastings, for The Lady Anne's.

Ollie Dalziel, David Walklate and Alan Abbott, for material from the twilight years.

David Carrington, for being a long-suffering 'critical friend'.

And all the characters, remembered or forgotten, who are woven into the rich tapestry portraying the life of this remarkable sportsman.

Bibliography

Books

Addis, Ian, Dean, Mick and Slough, Brian, *Brian Reynolds: The Times and Life of the Northamptonshire Sportsman* (Diametric, 2000)

Agnew, Jonathan, *Cricket: A Modern Anthology* (Harper Collins, 2013)

Brearley, Mike, *The Art of Captaincy* (Hodder and Stoughton, 1985)

Brown Edge Memories (Churnet Valley Books, 2008)

Chalke, Stephen, *Guess My Story: The Life and Opinions of Keith Andrew, Cricketer* (Fairfield, 2003)

Duckworth, L, *SF Barnes: Master Bowler* (The Cricketer/Hutchinson, 1967)

Engel, Matthew (ed.), *The Guardian Book of Cricket* (Penguin, 1987)

Engel, Matthew and Radd, Andrew, *The History of Northamptonshire County Cricket Club* (Helm, 1993)

Kent, Jeff, *The Valiants' Years: The Story of Port Vale* (Witan Books, 1990)

Menon Suresh, *Bishan: Portrait of a Cricketer* (Penguin, 2011)

Northamptonshire CCC Year Book (Various)

Northamptonshire County League Handbook (Various)

Priestley, JB, *English Journey* (Heinemann , 1934)

Radd, Andrew, *Northamptonshire County Cricket Club: 100 Greats* (History Press, 2001)

Radd, Andrew, *Northamptonshire County Cricket Club: Fifty of the Finest Matches* (History Press, 2002)

South African Cricket Annual (Various)

Steele, David, and Morris, J, *Come In Number Three* (Pelham Books, 1977)

Swanton, EW, *Barclays World of Cricket* (HarperCollins, 1980)

Wisden Cricketers' Almanack (Wisden, Various)

Magazines

Cricketer International, The Cricketer, Wisden Cricket Monthly

INDEX

216

Also from Chequered Flag Publishing:

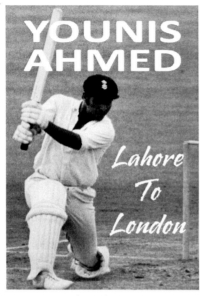

Lahore To London

by Younis Ahmed

Younis Ahmed was a talented, attacking middle-order batsman who left his native Pakistan to forge a successful career in cricket around the globe. But he is not remembered for his vibrant batting. Instead it is for moments of controversy: an international ban for touring apartheid-era South Africa, taking Surrey to a tribunal, leaving Worcestershire under a cloud. Now Younis tells his side of the story.

Younis also describes winning the County Championship and Quaid-e-Azam Trophy, replacing Garry Sobers at South Australia at the invitation of Don Bradman, pioneering professionalism and sponsorship in cricket, taking the sport to the Middle East and playing alongside legends including Javed Miandad and Imran Khan.

This is the colourful and chequered story of how one cricketer's journey from Lahore to London took him to the top of the game, but also to the depths of rejection and despair.

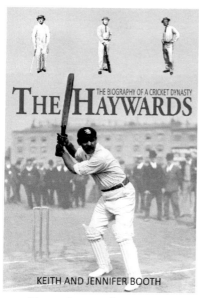

THE HAYWARDS

THE BIOGRAPHY OF A CRICKET DYNASTY

by Keith and Jennifer Booth

Four players, three generations, two counties, one famous family.

The mourners who attended the funeral of Daniel Hayward in 1852 lamented the loss of a fine cricketer, but little did they realise that his family would continue to star in English cricket for another 60 years. One son was a stalwart of Cambridgeshire cricket; the other would help pioneer and popularise cricket as a famous member of the All-England Eleven. A grandson would eclipse them all, becoming one of the greatest batsmen of all time and the second to score a century of centuries.

Together the Haywards featured in nearly 900 first-class or equivalent matches, scored nearly 50,000 runs and took over 750 wickets. They witnessed the growth of cricket from its early days as a pastime for gentlemen to an international sport with huge crowds. They took part in the first overseas cricket tour, spurred the rise of county cricket and battled for the Ashes.

Using extensive archival research, Keith and Jennifer Booth shine the spotlight on four fascinating characters, elevating the Hayward name to rank alongside Grace and Lillywhite as one of cricket's foremost families.

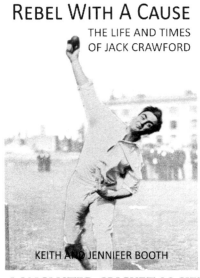

REBEL WITH A CAUSE

THE LIFE AND TIMES OF JACK CRAWFORD

by Keith and Jennifer Booth

LONGLISTED CRICKET SOCIETY & MCC BOOK OF THE YEAR 2017

Prodigy. Record breaker. Enigma.

Jack Crawford, described as the greatest ever schoolboy cricketer, blazed into the Surrey team at the age of seventeen and broke a host of records: the youngest Surrey centurion and double centurion, the youngest player to achieve the double of 100 wickets and 1,000 runs in a season. He became the youngest cricketer to play for England and a Wisden Cricketer of the Year.

Yet, not long after his twenty-first birthday, he played the last of his twelve Test matches. He fell out with the Surrey committee, then with the South Australian Cricket Association and Otago Cricket Association after moving to play in the Southern Hemisphere. What went wrong?

Crawford's career raises many questions which have only been partially answered. Why did he stand up to the Surrey committee? What happened in Australia and New Zealand? Did he try to dodge the Great War? Was he a bigamist? Now, thanks to Keith and Jennifer Booth's meticulous research, the truth is fully known.